"*I am sure that you will be encouraged and strengthened in faith, as I was, as you read how Rita and Norm have stood and fought against compromising their beliefs and giving in to tradition, in order to live out a vibrant witness for Christ before a lost and needy world. NO SHADOW OF TURNING is a powerful demonstration that God's laws do work, both in marriage and in successful careers.*"

From the *Foreword*
by Jim Bakker

Every good gift and every perfect gift is from above, and cometh down from the Father of lights, with whom is no variableness, neither shadow of turning.
—JAMES 1:17 (King James)

NO SHADOW OF TURNING

Norman and Rita Walter

with
PAM PROCTOR

SPIRE BOOKS

Fleming H. Revell Company
Old Tappan, New Jersey

ISBN 0-8007-8413-8
A Spire Book
Published by Fleming H. Revell Company
Originally Published by
Doubleday & Company, Inc.,
as a Doubleday-Galilee Original
Copyright © 1980 by Rita Walter, Norman E.
Walter, and Priscilla Proctor
All Rights Reserved
Printed in the United States of America

To our parents,
Sylvester and Anne McLaughlin
and Norman and Claire Walter,
who taught us early in life
the unchanging faithfulness of God.

FOREWORD

Honestly, when I first heard about them, I didn't believe it. An evangelical minister and a television soap-opera actress, happily married and each continuing to pursue their own careers in a spirit of unity. In getting to know Norm and Rita Walter, however, I discovered them to be a real and most courageous couple. Like the soap opera in which Rita stars, theirs is a love story, honest, touching, and victorious in Christ. I am sure that you will be encouraged and strengthened in faith, as I was, as you read how Rita and Norm have stood and fought against compromising their beliefs and giving in to tradition, in order to live out a vibrant witness for Christ before a lost and needy world. *No Shadow of Turning* is a powerful demonstration that God's laws do work, both in marriage and in successful careers.

—Jim Bakker

CONTENTS

1

"Could This Be Mr. Right?"

A little red brick house with a garden in front and a small back yard filled with tomato plants, vegetables, and a miniature pear tree—this was my home in Brooklyn, U.S.A.

From my earliest years, my life revolved around my family. My mom was the best cook in the world, my dad was my hero, and my two brothers were the greatest.

Every morning I'd wake up, put on my maroon uniform, and head for Mass at Sts. Simon and Jude Church before school started. I loved going to church—it was quiet and filled with the holy presence of God. After Mass I'd leave the large Gothic sanctuary and walk down the long steps just about ready to burst with the love of God.

Early in life I learned about God's love. Praying was as natural as talking to a close friend. Going to church on Sundays wasn't something my brothers and I had to do. It was something we wanted to do.

Most of it was my parents' influence. They would talk

about God with a respect and love that were genuine and contagious.

My father would worship with a beautiful enthusiasm. He would sit up straight in the pew with his eyes wide open and put himself wholeheartedly into the prayers and hymns—sometimes with twice the volume we thought he should.

Sunday afternoons meant being together. The house smelled of tomato sauce and meat balls from my mother's Italian kitchen. Around the table we were immediately caught up in family conversation and in passing homemade *cutziti*. And we were careful to pass the Parmesan cheese far from my dad's allergic Irish nose. The Sunday *News* and the New York *Times* would be spread around the house, and laughter would come from the front porch, where my dad would pass the afternoon with Dagwood and Beetle Bailey.

My mother was an orthodontist's assistant and would get home at 5 P.M. I'd be home by three and find a note waiting for me: "Dear Rita, hope you had a good day—put in potatoes at 4 P.M., fold socks, set table, do homework. See you later. Love, Mommy." Sometimes I'd wait till right before five to do my chores, and David and I would rush around the house trying to get them done. The real list came on Saturday morning —wash dishes, dust furniture, clean bathroom (my specialty). After I'd finish I'd rush outdoors to play filled with a strong sense of accomplishment and importance.

I'll always thank my mother for the way she taught us to feel for other people. If there was a neighbor who complained of the kids being too noisy, instead of talking against the woman to us, she'd explain why she was like that—maybe the woman had no children around and wasn't used to the noise. We were told to be extra quiet around her house and always to say a big hello to make her feel wanted. Instead of growing up thinking that teachers and neighbors were mean and out to get us, we learned that people deserved respect and concern and that you can overcome problems with kindness. Mom always had a curious mind—she read a lot and enjoyed the discussion shows on TV. She was the one who told us about the religious programs like those of Oral Roberts and Rex Humbard and was always open to hearing more of the Gospel.

What I remember most of all about my childhood were the parties we had. Mom would decorate our finished basement and bring out the food. My older brother, Joseph, who was a seminarian, would bring home lots of friends. He'd play the piano and we'd all stand around singing and laughing. I'd often tell my parents how great it was to be so rich. Dad would laugh because of the bills and the mortgage and his city job. But I told him, "If I can go to the refrigerator and get out anything that I want—we've got to be rich!"

Dad was superintendent of street lighting for the Borough of Queens and a lieutenant colonel in the Army Reserves.

If our fathers can give us a picture of our relationship with our heavenly Father, then I had the best model anyone could have had. My father was a moral man with tremendous character. He was always ready to help when someone called to say, "The oil burner broke down" or "We can't stop the leak." He was caring and selfless and, most important of all, loving. We always knew how much he loved us. He enjoyed helping us with our homework and he encouraged everything we did with his favorite expression, "I have the fullest confidence in you." Once when I was nervous before a test, I teased him, "If I fail this test, at least it'll be with the fullest confidence!"

My father was a beautiful Christian, but after I gave him a copy of *The Living Bible* his faith really soared. He devoured it. He read through it twice and loved to underline his favorite passages. Then at an Oral Roberts meeting his hand shot up enthusiastically when Oral asked people to recommit their lives to Christ. Dad was ecstatic and we all shared in the excitement of his faith.

About five years earlier, my father had had an injury on the job which gave him intense back pain and forced him to retire. With a back brace and painkillers, he lost his appetite and was getting worse. But thanks to my mother's efforts at good nutrition and her loving care, his health improved greatly. I was glad I had decided to move back home after graduating from college. Joseph had become a Catholic priest and was busy at a church in Queens, and my younger brother, David, a black belt in karate and a film maker, was away at Oral Roberts University. Left at home were just my parents and me, and we grew even closer.

Then suddenly, in 1975, my father started to lose weight. He couldn't digest his food and he had stomach pains. We took him to the hospital for three days of extensive tests.

"Your husband's going to be just fine," the doctor assured my mother that first day. "It's just a slight absorption problem."

Every day I went to the hospital in place of my mother, who was suffering from a bad knee. On my father's third day in the hospital, during evening visiting hours, I smiled and told him to move over because I was tired. I lay down next to him on the bed, hugged him, and gave him a kiss. As I lay there next to his frail, thin body, I could feel him overflow with love for everyone.

"I've got such a wonderful wife," he said. "And you're such a great daughter. And I'm so proud of Joseph and David."

As he talked, it seemed that he had gotten his life in order and was looking back on it. He then started to share excitedly about Jesus from an Oral Roberts book and told me how Joseph had stopped by that afternoon to give him communion and anoint him with oil in the prayer for the sick. Finally, the eight-o'clock bell went off, and it was time to leave.

Now Dad was an Army man and always followed rules to the letter. But this time he didn't want me to go and asked me to stay longer.

"They won't mind," he said. I stayed a few more minutes but then had to go. "I'm sorry, I have to leave, Dad. But I'll see you tomorrow."

He came back with a familiar response of his: "Don't be sorry, be happy!"

That night I said my prayers as usual and read through one of the daily blessing books that have an inspirational verse for each day. The verse that night was from Psalm 125: "Those who trust in the Lord are steady as Mount Zion, unmoved by any circumstance" (*The Living Bible*). I repeated the verse a few times, and went off to sleep.

I never have trouble sleeping, but that night I kept tossing and turning. It was a little after midnight when I woke up in a sweat. "Please, God, don't let my father die."

I couldn't stop crying. I gave God a list of reasons why I needed my father.

"He has to know the man I'm going to marry," I said. "And he has to hold his grandchildren." I couldn't go through these experiences without him—I just couldn't.

Then God spoke to me. He spoke in my mind, but it was as clear as if He had spoken aloud.

I stopped crying and listened in the dark with my eyes wide open.

"Don't you trust Me?" God said gently. "I *love* your father —far more than you ever could. Trust Me. I'm going to take care of everything."

At that moment, a tremendous sense of peace came over me. Dad was in God's hands, and though I wasn't sure what was going to happen, I knew everything would be okay. God loved my father and He would take care of him. Then it felt like an angel's soft hand was stroking me gently, and I drifted off into a deep sleep.

The phone rang at 2 A.M. My mother got there first, and after a moment she turned to me. "Daddy passed away."

It was the morning of December 8, 1975, and it felt like we were in a vacuum, being transported to another place. But then I remembered how God had spoken to me and I knew He was in control. We called Joseph, who immediately drove home. We waited a few hours to call David at school and he made arrangements to take the first flight home.

The morning of the wake I had to appear on "As the World Turns." God answered my prayer that I wouldn't break down in front of my friends at work when they offered their condolences.

God gave me this special opportunity to thank them for their love and tell them about His love. "We're Christians," I said, "and this is what we're preparing for—the day when we'll be home with God in heaven."

The next day after everyone had left the funeral parlor, and Joseph had gone ahead to church to prepare for the funeral Mass, David and I were alone with Mom. They were about to close the casket, but Mom was having a hard time letting Daddy go. After holding up so well, she was now beginning to fall apart, and quickly asked us to sing my father's favorite hymn, "Fill My Cup, Lord." While the pallbearers waited in the back of the room, David and I tried to sing the song with as much voice as would come out.

When we finished, we looked at Mom and a peaceful serenity had come over her face. She was able to get through the entire service that followed.

Joseph was the chief celebrant of the Mass and all vestments were in white. The Easter candle was brought out to symbolize Christ's resurrection. David read from the prophets and Psalms, I read from the Book of Corinthians, and Joseph read from the Gospel of John. The choir sang alleluias and it was truly a joyous celebration of my father's entry into heaven. The church was filled with relatives and such friends from the show as Kathy Hays and Patsy Bruder.

What could have seemed like very difficult days became a time when God drew me closer to Him. A trip to the Holy Land had to be canceled so I could have a double-hernia operation on March 8, my twenty-fifth birthday. I was very sick after the operation and had to be back to work one week later. Then I was selected "Azalea Queen" for the Azalea Festival of Wilmington, North Carolina. But I got the flu. I tried my best to make all the different activities and rested whenever I could.

The night of the coronation ceremony I was in the dressing room, my head pounding, my ears stuffed, and my mind trying to put together my acceptance speech, when there was a knock at the door. It was Richard and Patti Roberts. They were going to be singing that night with the World Action Singers.

"We heard you weren't feeling well. We'd like you to join us in our prayer time before we go on, if you feel up to it." When they prayed for me, my ears cleared and my head stopped hurting. I was able to face the hundreds of people in the audience and everything I had wanted to say came easily. I told them about God's love and healing. A lot had happened in the past few months, but God's presence was closer than ever, His comfort sweeter. Coronation night, April 10, would have been my father's sixtieth birthday, but God had better plans for him.

In the months that followed, God continued to make His presence clear to me. The time I felt it most was the weekend I visited a monastery in the country to meet a former actress who had become a nun. I was looking forward to sharing my faith with her because we had so much in common, and I was happy to be in the countryside, free to think of nothing but God.

When we met, she was behind a grated window. She had been working in the fields, and came in wearing a denim habit and not a touch of makeup. I was struck by her beauty, by the spirit of God which glowed within her.

As we talked, I told her about the opportunities I had as an actress to share my faith in soap opera articles, on Rev. Robert Schuller's "Hour of Power" TV show, and at an Oral Roberts seminar. She seemed interested and pleased. But when I saw her again the day I left, her attitude had changed.

"You'd better sit down," she said quietly. "I spoke to the Mother Superior and one of the other sisters about you, and there's something we have to tell you."

I leaned forward to catch every word and wondered what the problem could be.

"We all feel you are in danger of losing your faith."

Her words hit me like a boulder. I thought maybe God was telling me through her that I wasn't in fellowship with Him.

But then I realized that by "faith" she meant my Catholic faith.

"Is it because of my Protestant friends?" I asked.

"We feel you're walking a tightrope of your faith and that you've got to be very careful."

During the two-hour drive home, I replayed the conversation in my mind, and started to cry. I had had high anticipations for the weekend and wasn't prepared for what had happened.

But then, just as God had spoken to me the night of my father's death, He spoke to me again. In a loving but very strong voice He said, "Don't look for approval from anyone else but Me. You know what our relationship is. And you know that you are with Me." I was looking for a pat on the back or some kind of encouragement. But God wanted me to look only to Him.

His words "Don't look for approval from anyone else" have never left me. I didn't know then that these words, a few months later, would have tremendous meaning for me.

I hadn't seriously dated anyone for a couple of years, and, looking back, I thanked God that I had so much free time to take Bible classes, go to Christian concerts, and develop strong Christian friendships. But I also knew that I wanted to find that special person that I could love and share my life with.

The crew at CBS are a great group and they knew how much I wanted to get married. Sometimes I'd bring a date to the studio and the next day they'd ask, "How about him?"

"No, he's not the one," I'd say. "I think I've just been too spoiled with a man like my father."

They'd tell me I was too selective and I'd never find the right guy. Every now and then, friends would say, "I've got the perfect person for you. He's a doctor, he's young, he's good-looking, and he has a great personality."

Well, I'd meet him, and we'd have a good time, but there was always something missing. In the eyes of the world we might have been a good match, but I knew we just weren't right for each other.

But one concerned friend said frankly, "Rita, if you ever do get a guy, I think you're going to have problems. God means so much to you, your husband's going to be jealous."

But I knew that only when God lives in your heart can you really begin to overflow with love for others, especially for your husband.

Often, somebody at work would ask me, "What are you so happy about?" especially when we started work at 7 A.M. I'd smile and say, "Oh, I'm in love with someone and He loves me."

"Who is it?" the person would ask. One day, C. David Colson, who was playing my husband on "As the World Turns," heard the question and answered for me.

"It's God," he said with a smile, and walked on. I wondered about the kind of man who could marry someone like me.

"If he's a Christian, which I'd really like, he probably won't understand my being an actress," I thought. "And if he's an actor, he probably won't understand my Christian faith."

I thought that I had come up with a job that was too tough for even God to handle! I'd try to keep my sense of humor: "Lord, please hurry, I'm beginning to lose interest. I've almost forgotten how Saturday nights can be different." Oh, I could date—just to go out with someone. And when I was a teenager I dated a lot. But now that I was older, if the person didn't seem like the type I might marry, I just couldn't keep dating him.

Every time I'd start to get impatient, I'd remind myself what it would be like to be married to the wrong person. I knew it'd be better to be single than to make the wrong choice. "And then again," I thought, "maybe God has somebody in mind for me when I'm thirty-three. There's no sense worrying for eight years until I meet him." So I rested in that fact and trusted that "Father knows best."

Spring of '76 was just turning to summer, and each day brought with it a deeper sense that something great was about to happen. I didn't understand it, but it made me feel excited. I would say over and over again to my friend Marsha Clark (who now plays Hillary on another CBS soap opera, "The Guiding Light"), "I don't know what's going to happen, but I just know that this is going to be the greatest summer ever."

Soon I got the chance to attend The Christian Booksellers Association Convention in Atlantic City, New Jersey. I had read several books by Charles and Frances Hunter, and when I saw them at a booth on the convention floor, I went over to introduce myself.

"I just wanted to tell you how much I've enjoyed your books, especially on marriage," I told them.

Frances Hunter smiled warmly and said, "Oh, are you married?"

"No," I said.

"Are you engaged?"

"No, I'm not. There's no one in sight right now, but when the time comes, I'll be ready!"

Before I could say another word, she put her hands on my shoulders, closed her eyes, and in a loud, strong voice prayed, "O heavenly Father, we ask You to bring into this woman's life the exact man You have for her. He will be the perfect person for her, and pick her like a rose out of a garden. And they will know without a shadow of a doubt that they are for each other. In Jesus' name, we pray. Amen."

I was deeply moved by her spontaneous prayer, and I couldn't help feeling assured that God would answer that prayer—someday.

It was just the next week when my friends Steve and Terrie Bolster (Steve had played Mark Galloway on "As the World Turns") said, "We want you to meet our pastor, Reverend Norman Walter." Steve drew a map to their church and on it he wrote:

"This is the way to your future husband."

2

"It's Just One Date"

To my left, the sky was streaked with the red and gold of sunset. In the distance were the lights of homes settling down for a normal evening. Somehow, I knew that for me this evening would be anything but normal.

On my right I could see the skyline of New York. From the time my parents took us to Macy's and the automat on Christmas Eve, New York was to me an exciting city on the edge of forever. If a dream could ever come true, I always believed it would happen there.

This was a great time in my life because God had already accomplished the greatest goal I had set for myself. All I had ever really wanted to be was a minister. I knew it would be wrong to take personal pride in the "Rev." before my name, but I felt a deep inner confidence in who I was. Pastoring my church in New Jersey was more important than money or even a family. As a matter of fact, I was afraid to even talk about marriage because I felt it might affect my career.

But now I was on the Jersey Turnpike on my way to a blind date with a TV star. My date with Rita McLaughlin had been set up by Steve and Terrie Bolster, members of my new congregation. When I watched Rita on "As the World Turns" she was as pretty as he had told me she was. A few days before, Steve and I were standing on the church lawn, changing the signboard. He smiled and said, "I know you're really going to like Rita. But I must tell you one thing—she's Catholic."

My heart sank. Any girl a minister dated would be thoroughly scrutinized by the congregation, and I already knew what some of the reaction would be to this.

Well, the date was already made. And after all, one date wasn't going to change my whole life. Besides, I really wanted to meet her.

When I got near the block in Manhattan where Rita was staying, I discovered I was an hour early. So I pulled over to the side of the street to wait. But accidentally, I dozed off. I woke up later thinking I had slept too long. I looked at my watch and was relieved to find that I still had a few minutes left. I practically ran all the way to the building.

My heart was pounding in anticipation as I walked up to the doorman and asked him to ring the apartment. The wait seemed endless. Then he looked up blankly from the phone. There was no one home.

"Well," I thought. "I might have expected something like this." Then I remembered the address book where I had scribbled a few other numbers she had given me. I called them all and got nothing but a continuous ring.

Just as I was about to give up, a car pulled up in front of the building. Out of the sudden confusion of doormen and people moving through the revolving doors—there she was. Everyone else seemed to disappear. All I could focus on was an angelic vision with a soft smile walking toward me.

Our hands met in a moment of greeting, and it was like no other moment of my life. Everything said that this beautiful girl was more special than the rest. We stood in the apartment lobby smiling at each other for a few seconds.

Then we were in the midst of excited introductions. There were her mother, Anne, her brothers, David and Joseph, who were helping Rita move into a friend's apartment for a few weeks. As the rest of the family headed for the elevator carrying her suitcases and bags of food, Rita turned to me.

"It's always been a tradition in my family that on the first date my family goes with me," she said.

"That's all right with me," I said deadly seriously, noticing the gleam in her eye.

There was something about her that immediately set me at ease. Just a few minutes earlier I had thought she wouldn't show up for the date. And now the look of comfort and warmth in her eyes relaxed me completely.

We stood alone in the elevator, just looking at each other and smiling. There was no need for idle conversation about the weather or what we did that day. There was an unspoken rapport between us that seemed to say everything.

Rita's mother was in the kitchen putting groceries away, and Joseph was sitting at the piano playing softly when we walked in. A few minutes later, Rita put a glass of apple juice in my hand and we were talking about health food and nutrition at the dining room table.

For about twenty minutes we talked about our work. And Rita was full of questions. I explained to her that I had a monthly radio show and that I had just become pastor of a new congregation. It was a free-flowing conversation, with none of the normal hesitations of a first date. Somehow, it seemed like we had known each other for a long, long time.

Every now and then her mother would drop into the conversation. And once she said something that kind of puzzled me.

"Joseph doesn't know you're a minister," she said, almost in a whisper.

I wasn't quite sure how to respond, so I let it drop.

"Nothing can go wrong tonight," I thought, looking at Rita. "Here I am in New York City, with a beautiful girl. It's like something out of a storybook."

It was getting late and at seven-thirty we had planned to meet Steve and Terrie Bolster. We were to meet them at the Lamb's Club, a Christian supper club run by the Manhattan Church of the Nazarene, near Times Square. The building had once been the theatrical gathering place of Broadway and Hollywood celebrities, and it seemed appropriate that I was going there now escorting a Christian celebrity.

As we drove to the Lamb's, we felt so free to talk that I couldn't resist asking a question that had been bothering me since we had left the apartment.

"What did your mother mean when she said your brother Joseph didn't know I was a minister?" I asked. "What line of work is he in?"

"He's a priest," Rita said, with the faintest, knowing smile.

"Oh," I said, trying to appear nonchalant. But in the back of my mind I was reminded again about the reaction of my new Baptist congregation.

Our conversation was so free and easy that I wanted it to go on forever. Rita obviously did too. "I almost wish we weren't going there tonight," she said. "I wish we could just keep talking."

We arrived at the Lamb's ten minutes late because I went down the wrong block, and Steve and Terrie were waiting for us in the lobby. The four of us went upstairs to the big dining room and sat at a large table with several people we didn't know. We were all in high spirits as we introduced ourselves, and I was wondering what response people would have to meeting Rita. After all, she was a nationally famous TV star. But surprisingly enough, the first person the people at our table recognized was me. Some of the ladies sitting with us had never seen "As the World Turns," so they didn't know Rita or Steve. But they were faithful followers of my local radio show!

It didn't take long, however, for me to shatter my "celebrity" image. I was about to dig into the meal when I discovered that my maroon tie was in the salad and was smeared with blue cheese dressing. I looked up and saw Steve and Terrie trying not to notice.

"Oh great," I thought. But then I overheard Rita turn to Terrie and whisper, "I like this guy. He's just like me."

Before I knew it, she had taken her napkin and was wiping the dressing from my tie. It was such an intimate gesture that by the time she finished wiping it off I was glad the whole thing had happened.

One thing I had never gotten straight about Rita was her age. When I saw her on TV, she looked older than I. And somehow, when I looked in the mirror as I was getting ready for the date, I looked my youngest. I was sure she would be older, especially since my mother said she had been on the show for seven years.

Rita was wondering the same thing about me. She said, "By the way, how old are you?"

"Twenty-eight," I said.

"You're *so young*," she said in surprise. That did it. I was sure she was at least ten years older.

"How old are you?" I asked somewhat tentatively.

"Twenty-five."

I relaxed. She said she thought I must be in my thirties to be so "mature." Everything seemed perfect.

After dinner we went upstairs to the Lamb's theater to see a series of Gospel vignettes.

We sat there watching the show, laughing and talking between skits and clapping enthusiastically. I decided to play it low-key with Rita and not come on too strong. I didn't want to scare her away. But I was dying to have the program end, so we could say good night to Steve and Terrie, leave the crush of people, and be alone.

But after the show, people started milling around Rita, talking to her, asking for her autograph. A few times her fans pulled her away from me. But in the midst of all these people, Rita reached over and grabbed my arm saying, "Come here, Norman, I want you to meet someone."

At one point the press of fans became too great and Rita disappeared from me for a minute. I found myself talking to an attractive young woman who said she was a stewardess. She was friendly, and I didn't want to appear rude, but I couldn't help wondering what Rita would think.

My fears were short-lived, and soon we were back together and heading for the door. We said goodbye to our friends and headed for the car.

"Do you want to take a ride on the Staten Island ferry?" I asked, thinking that the ferry was one of the most romantic rides I knew.

"Well, it's kind of late," she said, smiling and squinting at me with those eyes I would grow to love so quickly. "Why don't we just walk?" So I drove up to Columbus Circle and parked the car near Central Park.

The city was its most dazzling. It was a clear, bright night, and we could even see the stars. The lights of Manhattan sparkled like jewels against the velvet darkness of the park. The traffic was subdued, and often we could hear the sound of horses' hooves from the carriages passing us along Central Park South.

Rita thought it would be fun to take a horse and carriage ride, and since she had a girl friend who drove one, she stopped at a phone booth to call and find out if her friend was on duty. As she was talking, she noticed a thread on my shirt and started to twirl the thread around a button. When she hung up and said that her friend wasn't working, I slowly, carefully slipped my hand in hers and we started walking.

The touch of her hand was warm and comfortable. And I was again struck by the feeling that this evening and this girl were somehow different from the rest.

We walked for a couple of hours up Fifth Avenue along the park. We couldn't find out enough about each other, and there was an instant oneness between us.

And I couldn't get over her openness. At one point she looked at me and said sweetly, "You have such a nice smile."

I thought, "It takes such freedom to be able to say that to someone. Usually people on first dates are tense, want to seem sophisticated and don't want to appear vulnerable. So they put up a front." Instead, Rita was natural and unaffected.

"I want to know this girl better," I said to myself, as I gazed at her beautiful face, with her tender eyes looking up at me.

It was one or two in the morning when we decided to head back to her apartment. I had a sermon to deliver the next day, and I thought I should get Rita home. I drove her back, and we got in the elevator holding hands and thinking our own private thoughts.

I had never spent an evening with anyone on TV and I had never dated a girl quite like Rita. I sure didn't want to ruin it. And I didn't want to hear from Steve in church the next day that his minister had made an unwanted advance. The last thing I wanted to do was offend Rita. But then again, I was certainly willing to let a romantic situation develop.

So I stood there at the door, trying to be sensitive to what she wanted, waiting for some sign.

"I had a great time," she told me. With that, she extended her hand.

"I have my sign," I thought. As much as I would have loved to kiss her good night, I was relieved that at least the signal was clear.

I shook her hand and started to back away toward the elevator. But Rita didn't let go. She held onto my hand and pulled me back toward her. Then she reached up and whispered in my ear, "Do ministers kiss on the first date?"

"Yes, they do," I said. I leaned over until our lips softly touched.

In four days I would ask her to be my wife.

3

"The Making of an Actress"

One day after school when I was nine years old, I slipped into one of the long wooden pews in the almost empty church near my home in Brooklyn. I knelt down and talked with God the way we had so many times before.

But this time, I asked God right out, "Do You want me to be a nun?"

I knew you had to feel a calling from God, and I wanted to know what He wanted me to be. My brother Joseph was giving his life to God, studying to be a priest. And one of my teachers, Sister Michaeleen, seemed to glow from within. I also wanted to respond to God's love in a deep way.

I waited for some response from God—some kind of inner knowing that would confirm my request. Instead, I felt nothing. It wasn't a blank emptiness, but a purposeful silence that hit me with a response I wasn't ready for. I couldn't understand why God didn't want me to be a nun. And I continued to tell Him how I wanted people to know about Him, how

He loved them and wanted to fill their lives with His peace and joy. But His answer was still "no" and it was hard to accept.

As I sat back in the pew, I tried to think what else I could become. A nurse? No, I felt faint too easily. Maybe a teacher. "Yes, I suppose that's what You want me to become, Lord, a teacher," I said.

Before I left the church, I added: "If You ever change Your mind, God, just let me know. I'll be waiting."

I knew that someday God would let me know what my calling would be. But what I didn't realize was that His calling would take me to a world that was far different from my familiar world of going to school and playing punchball with the other kids on the block.

About a year after I offered my prayer in church, God started me on a path toward TV as an actress—a role that I could never have imagined for myself.

My first steps on the path toward an acting career had actually started when I was five years old, in the form of dancing lessons. I had always been very shy, and my mom thought that dancing lessons might help draw me out of myself. Off we went to a local dancing school—the kind with recitals and bright sequined outfits that my Aunt Josie would make. It was all so much fun, and I really loved it—tap dancing, ballet—everything. In fact, I was doing so well that my dance teacher suggested I take lessons at the June Taylor dancing school in Manhattan, whose dancers were on "The Jackie Gleason Show."

Every Saturday, my brother Joseph would accompany me to Manhattan, and I'd take four classes in a row. There was ballet from Richard Thomas, the father of Richard Thomas of the TV program "The Waltons." After that there were acrobatics, then jazz, and then my favorite, tap. When the classes were finished, Joseph and I would go to the corner drugstore for a chocolate malted before the long train ride home.

But the lessons were just the beginning. The next step was a dance competition, sponsored by the city's Catholic Youth

Organization. Hundreds of girls from all over the city were competing, and I found myself winning the first round, then the second, and the third, until I was one of three finalists from the entire city.

Although my dance was a simple soft-shoe, my teacher worked with me on specific arm movements and style. And my mother gave me the best advice of all. "You've got to make the audience feel at ease. There's nothing wrong with being afraid. Just put your feelings in your pocket!"

As I stood in the wings, waiting to go onstage to dance in the finals, I could hear my mother saying, "Reach out and show them you love them."

That's exactly what I did. And it wasn't hard. I enjoyed dancing and I could feel that joy being transferred to the audience.

But just when I was ready to kick my right leg in a big finish, my left foot slipped on the highly polished floor and I landed flat on my behind. I was dazed for a second, then I bounced right up and landed—this time as planned—on one knee, with my hands outstretched and a big smile on my face. More than anything, I wanted the audience to feel that I was okay.

It was down to three of us when I heard them call my name. I won first place, a gold crown on an eight-pound plaque, and my first publicity article in the New York *World-Telegram:* "Rita has Hayley Mills beaten by a smile."

My dance teacher felt that I had the right personality to do commercials and suggested that my mother get me an agent. It all seemed so remote, so impossible. But my mother was adventurous and it sounded like it could be fun. "Why not give it a try?" She bought several of the trade papers such as *Variety* and *Backstage*, looked up a list of agents, and pointed the car toward Manhattan.

"Make sure this is something you really want to do," she told me. "It will take a lot of time and energy, and you have to be sure it's what you want to do."

I nodded my head in anticipation, and off we went.

At the first agency, the woman in charge took one look at me with my thick eyeglasses and said, "I'm sorry, but we have the cream of the crop here." My heart sank. I thought, "I guess this isn't for me."

But my mother had great spirit. "Since we came all the way in, why don't we just try one more agency. It can't hurt." Mom has always taught us to have a sense of humor and not take ourselves too seriously, and she could always make a situation brighter.

So we went to the next agency on our list, only to find that they had just closed for the day. But for some reason, the receptionist took a liking to us. She said I was the *Sound of Music* type, and ran back to one of the agents, saying, "I've got just one more girl for you to see."

This time I didn't wear my glasses. I walked in half blind and smiled. And this time I got a big smile in return. "You're just perfect for commercials!" the agent said.

That made me feel great. We left the agency on top of the world. But even then my mother was very wise. She took the woman's enthusiasm with a grain of salt, not wanting me to be disappointed if nothing ever came through.

Once a friend of mine was up for a commercial, and before she went out to audition her mother said, "You get that commercial for us—we really could use that money."

I would have died if I had had that kind of pressure. For me, the world of commercials and show business was a great experience. It wasn't a career. It was just something I did on the side while I was going to school preparing to be a teacher. Or so I thought.

The agency that had been so enthusiastic about me didn't call back, so my mother decided to take the initiative and call them.

"You called just in time," said the agent. "The science show 'Watch Mr. Wizard' is auditioning eleven-year-old girls, and I'd like to send Rita along to try out."

Off I went to Manhattan again, this time chaperoned by my brother Joseph, one of the show's biggest fans. As I sat in the office waiting to be called, I asked the girl next to me whether she had ever done TV before. She reeled off a whole string of TV programs, acting jobs, and commercials she had done.

I thought, "I don't know what I'm doing here—I'll never get this, but it's fun anyway."

Just as my name was called for the audition, I thought, "God, please help me do a good job."

I made it past the first interviewer, who told me that the show was informal, without a script, and that I was to act like the girl next door who drops in on Mr. Wizard for an interesting science lesson. My role was that of the child at home watching the show and reacting as he or she would to the experiments. Then I got called back to meet Mr. Wizard, Don Herbert, an easygoing man I'd seen so often on TV, and he made me feel very relaxed.

For the audition, Mr. Wizard did a series of experiments. Several people, including the director, assistant director, and a science consultant from New York University, watched me interact with Mr. Wizard, taking notes on my temperament and responses. I thanked God for my poor eyesight—I can only see clearly things that are less than a foot away. You can't be frightened by what you can't see!

First I had to put my hand, palm up, over a box, while Mr. Wizard put iron filings in my hand.

"That's heavy," I exclaimed. He put a few more in my hand.

"It's getting heavier." I said. "Is there a magnet in there by any chance?" Sure enough, there was.

"Tell me, Rita, how do you make rain?" he asked next. I thought for a minute. "A hot cloud meets a cold cloud and—pow—you have rain," I said, pounding my hands together.

Mr. Wizard laughed and I really felt good about the rest of the audition. I knew I could never get the job—there were more than two hundred girls auditioning—so the pressure was off and I was able to enjoy every moment.

A few days later, as I came up the back steps to our house

after riding my bike, my mother was just hanging up the phone.

"You got it!" she said excitedly. "You're going to play Mr. Wizard's assistant on NBC!"

I couldn't believe it. It seemed impossible. I was so grateful to God and I couldn't stop thanking Him.

For the next three years I did the show, alternating every week with a boy who played the same role. Along with getting a background in science, I learned all about television production and how to feel comfortable around live TV cameras.

Then I landed a spot on "Sing Along with Mitch." I had a cousin who worked at the NBC studios that happened to be near my home in Brooklyn. He had often asked us to stop by, so one day my mother suggested that I take an orange cake that I had baked to the studio. I did, and gave Mitch Miller a slice.

"How old are you?" he asked me.

"Thirteen," I answered.

"You're thirteen, I'm thirty-nine—that would be a perfect match."

I laughed. "I'm fully in favor of mixed marriages."

He set up an audition for me to dance, and the next week I was on the show as a regular. I was also featured in a tap dance as "Rosie O'Grady," while the "Mitchmen" dressed as Irish cops sang and danced along with me.

It was really through commercials, though, that I started to learn more about acting. I did Hi-C Orange Drink, Prell Shampoo, Thomas's English Muffins. It was all so exciting. I'll never forget my first commercial audition at the posh J. Walter Thompson advertising agency for Hi-C. I was dressed all in pink—pink sweater, pink skirt, pink knee socks, and a pink bow in my hair. I rode up in the elevator awestruck by New York and by the luxurious offices I went into. Next to me at the audition was a girl who was also eleven years old.

"Did you ever do a commercial?" I asked with wide eyes.

"Oh, I've done more than thirty," she said. I asked her

which ones and she rattled off a list of products but said she had forgotten a lot of them.

I thought, "Oh, dear God. If I ever get a commercial, I'll *never* forget a thing that happens."

Well, a week later, I learned that I had gotten the commercial. I was so excited I raced down the block and said to my girl friend, "I got the Hi-C commercial. I got it!" It was such a big moment for me, but she just shrugged. "So what?"

From that moment on, I decided it would be better to keep my work to myself and not talk about it. I didn't want to be different from the rest of the kids, even though I was falling in love with this new world. I didn't know then that I'd get to do more than a hundred commercials, and that just like that other girl I'd forget a lot of them too!

When it came time for me to start high school, I was working on commercials and on "Mr. Wizard." And although I wanted to go to a parochial school in Brooklyn, the principal suggested that I go to a professional children's high school where I would be like the other kids who were combining school with a career.

I enrolled at the Lincoln Square Academy, right across from Lincoln Center for the Performing Arts at Broadway and Sixty-fifth Street. Since it was a new school, the classes were small and there were only five in my freshman year. We were a close group and school spirit was high. "LSA, all the way!"

My parents were great listeners, and when I got home they would hear a full report on what Miss Melvin said in science class or what Mr. Schwartz said in math. Teachers understood when we had to be absent for work, as did other students who were often at the same auditions.

In one way I was like the other kids now. But in another way everything was different. When I was growing up, all the kids I knew in the neighborhood were Irish or Italian Catholics. In my new school I was thrown in with kids from all religious backgrounds—and mostly from none at all. It was hard for me to believe that they not only didn't know that God loved them—they didn't seem to care.

For the first time I was forced to be on my own and stand up for what I believed, and I remembered how the priests at my confirmation had taught that through the power of the Holy Spirit we were all soldiers for Christ.

Every now and then, I'd get a chance to tell one of the other kids that God loved them. And I felt an awesome sense of responsibility to tell them about Him. "If they don't know God, what's going to happen to them?" It seemed so easy for them to accept His love if only they knew about it.

One fellow in class, who was later in the movie *The Lords of Flatbush,* used to tease me and call me "Sister Rita." But not everyone joked about it. One day I was talking to a friend who had a problem. "Don't worry about it," I said. "You know God loves you no matter what happens." Another student happened to overhear our conversation and walked over to me angrily.

"You're so full of ——," he said.

I was shocked. There's a part of me that wants to be liked by other people, and for the first time my faith had caused a negative reaction. It made me think of Jesus and all the rejection and pain He had willingly suffered for my sins. I knew that Jesus loved that student and wanted to heal his hurts. If only that student had known it too.

During high school, I kept up a busy routine. I'd take three subways each way to school, go on auditions, do occasional radio or TV commercials, and try to fit in a dance class when I could. I joined the school choir and enjoyed playing softball in Central Park where Mr. Bevan, our physical education teacher, taught me "how *not* to pitch like a girl." I was also very active in my church. I played guitar at the Folk Mass, taught confraternity (religion) classes to second-graders, and went to my own classes along with singing in the teen-age and adult choirs.

Being an actress was still something I did "on the side," and I'd still tell people I was going to be a teacher. Besides, a real actress did heavy dramatic roles, crying scenes, and Shakespeare. The parts I played just stressed "being natural."

It never consciously entered my mind to make acting a career goal. But God was directing my career as I went along. He was my acting coach, and though I didn't take acting classes, I did have "on the job" training. Each new job became more and more difficult and I would encounter new directors, new characters to portray, new emotions to project, and new scripts and techniques to learn.

There are three specific times I had valuable acting lessons that I'll never forget. The first was on a TV program, "Faith for Today." My character was to be upset at the dinner table and have a bad headache.

Well, there I was with my face contorted into what I felt was a horrible headache, when the director came up to me and said, "Rita, have a worse headache—but don't show it."

"Don't show it," I learned. Emotion has to come from the inside out. If I feel it, it will get me across without any conscious movement of my face.

The second time, my brother David was in the role of director. He'd go over my lines with me and in one particular scene I had to be very angry. My brow was furrowed, my lips were tight—oh boy, was I mad.

In the past, sometimes directors would say, "Be natural" or "You're not feeling it," and I couldn't understand what they meant. After all, I *was* feeling it, and at this moment I felt angry and it had to be right.

But David could see that I was playing the scene all wrong. He was frank. "Why are you doing that with your eyebrows? You never look like that when you're yelling at me."

I looked in the mirror and saw what he meant. When I relaxed my facial muscles and just let the anger seethe inside me, I almost frightened me!

The third time I learned a key acting lesson was a few years later on "As the World Turns." The man who played my father, Ed Bryce, told me that the most important acting technique he had been taught was "to listen." "Listen intently to what the other character is saying to you, don't think about your next line or your emotion. Open up, be sensitive, and listen." This was all valuable advice I was gaining to make future scenes really work.

Through a series of TV roles—as Patty Duke's stand-in on "The Patty Duke Show," where I grew to admire her tremendously, and on several "Look Up and Live" episodes, I was gradually building my confidence as an actress.

And I was also learning more about God.

Even though I was taught that God's love is unconditional, I still believed that if I were good I might get a certain job, but if I had done something wrong, forget it. That's what was on my mind after I auditioned for the soap opera "The Secret Storm."

I was very nervous about the audition. This could be my first big dramatic part. I was fifteen, and although the audition had gone well, I was very unsure about the results. Earlier that week I had gotten into an argument with my mother, and although it was over and I was sorry, I knew I didn't deserve to get the job. So after the audition, when we got home, I threw myself on my bed and resigned myself to the outcome. "That's okay, I know I won't get it."

As I lay there, my mother knocked on the door and peeked in. " 'Secret Storm' called. You've got the part," she said.

I thought to myself, "They've got to be wrong. I'm not supposed to get that job."

But there were the facts—"You've got the part of Wendy Porter."

I said to myself, "How can God be so good?" And it hit me that His love wasn't dependent on how good I was. I didn't have to earn it. He loved me and was good to me when I least deserved it.

I became a regular on "The Secret Storm," but the part lasted for only three months. The producer decided to spice up the story line and sent my character away to college so she could come back an older girl.

But during those three months on the show, I had gained a fast dose of acting experience. I was so grateful for my years on "Mr. Wizard" and my experience doing a live show. God always took me along step by step. Of course, that didn't preclude my making mistakes, and I made a whopper on "Secret Storm."

Once I was supposed to refuse a drink and order tea instead, saying, "I'm a teetotaler." But in the script it was printed "teetilator." During rehearsal the director corrected me.

"It's teetotaler," she said.

For the next few hours I repeated, "Teetotaler, teetotaler," but sure enough, when we were on live TV and the hostess asked me if I'd like a drink, I said with a smile, "Oh no, thank you, I'm a tee-tilator!"

Well, everyone in the scene burst out laughing, and on live TV there's no chance for a retake. I was mortified. After the show I walked behind the set, hoping that the floor would open so I could just disappear through it!

Although God may close one door, he soon opens another. A few months after I left "Secret Storm" I got a part in my first Broadway play, *A Warm Body*, starring Kevin McCarthy and Dina Merrill. Hedy Lamarr's son, Tony Loder, played my boy friend and previews took us to the Royal Poincianna Playhouse in Palm Beach.

Dina Merrill left the play before it opened on Broadway, but meeting her and her husband, Cliff Robertson, was one of the highlights of my life. On opening night in Florida, Cliff knocked on my dressing room door and gave me a beautiful bouquet of flowers. I just about fainted.

Dina and Cliff made me feel so special. She was wonderful to work with, very warm and caring. On my sixteenth birthday, we were at the Paper Mill Playhouse in Millburn, New Jersey. My mother surprised me with a between-shows birthday party in my balloon-and-streamer-decorated dressing room. At the party Dina handed me a small, wrapped box. Inside was a shining gold medal, from Tiffany's, of St. Genesius, the patron saint of actors. I was speechless. Inscribed on the back were the words "To Rita, With Love, Cliff and Dina."

I'll always be proud to be in a profession where there are such beautiful people as the Robertsons.

The play finally came to Broadway for three weeks of previews at the Cort Theatre. On opening night, Walter Kerr from the New York *Times* was there to review it. Although the play closed immediately afterward, Kerr's review mentioned three actors by name—and I was one of them. "Rita McLaughlin is pretty as can be as the niece who means to get on the town as quickly as possible."

A few months later I got the chance I had always dreamed of. I was asked to fly to Hollywood to make a screen test for a Walt Disney movie. It was the first time Mom and I had ever flown first class to California and I felt like a fairytale princess. Disney never did make the movie, but I have beautiful memories of my visit there and still stop by the Walt Disney Studios whenever I'm in California.

While I was in Hollywood, I met an agent who was very enthusiastic about my future. After hearing good reports of my auditions, he insisted I stay in California to make the rounds and perhaps even get the bump on my nose fixed—for I was destined for "stardom."

Well, I was also destined to take my college boards back home, so back I went to New York, bump and all, to take my boards, finish high school, and graduate as Class of '68 valedictorian. In September I entered Marymount Manhattan College.

The following summer I won the lead in a pre-Broadway play called *Christabel and the Rubicon.* That's where I got an intense dose of stage experience. I was onstage for almost the entire show and had to do lengthy monologues and dramatic crying scenes.

The summer the show appeared, however, I was hit by the worst hayfever spell I've ever had. On opening night at the theater in Olney, Maryland, instead of relaxing before the show I was in bed, wearing a hat, thermal underwear, a sweater, and socks. I looked like I would never make it. I was sneezing my way through my third box of tissues, but with orange juice, rest, and lots of prayer, I revived enough that night to go on.

It felt so good to hear people laugh at our lines. The audience loved it. Later on at the opening night party, I was introduced to Richard Coe, the famed critic of the Washington *Post*, whose review we were most concerned about. I gave a slight bow and said, "This is such an honor."

With a gallant sweep of his arm, he bowed even lower than I and said, "Oh no, the honor is all mine. You were magnificent." In his review he described me as "a beguiling little redhead who revels in the long part . . . She can take pride in delivering so crisp a performance from a two-week rehearsal period." Those words kept me going through the days and weeks that followed, when I alternated between bed by day and the stage at night.

Before the summer, I had finished up a year at Marymount, commuting from my home in Brooklyn to school in Manhattan. And because the play had taken a lot out of me my parents suggested that I take a year off from school to rest, which I did. That's when I got the break of a lifetime—the chance to audition for the top soap opera "As the World Turns." The part was that of the girl friend of a young student named Tom Hughes.

The audition was agonizing. I was called back three times, and each time the field of actresses was narrowed further. But each time the wait between call-backs stretched for longer and longer periods—a week or more at a time. Finally, the part was down to two of us, a blonde, Kathleen Cody, and me.

Kathleen got the part. I was disappointed, but I told myself that if God had wanted me to get it I would have. "He must have other plans for me."

The following summer, the writers of the program decided to age Tom a few years and they wanted him to have a new girl friend, whose name was Carol Deming. Again I auditioned. And again it came down to two of us, a blonde and me. Each of us read opposite Tom, so the producers could match us together. This time I got it.

It's funny how your life can change with one turn. One minute they don't want you and you're far from being on the show, and the next minute they do want you and you're discussing contracts.

Now I was Carol, and it was too good to be true. The years on "As the World Turns" were filled with excitement. I was going to college in the afternoon and living at home in Brooklyn. Mom would have breakfast ready for me when I got up at six in the morning to go to work, and as I walked out the door she'd hand me a lunch bag. Along with fixing something nutritious, she would always write me a short note on the napkin, asking God to bless my day and telling me how much she cared.

During the winter months, Dad insisted on getting up early to warm up the car for me. Then I'd zip off to Manhattan in my red Mustang to spend the morning working at the studio. First the director blocked the scene so we knew when and where to sit or walk; then we'd run through the scene once with the cameras so they'd know what shots to take; then there was a run-through as a rehearsal, and then a dress rehearsal. Finally, from one to one-thirty, we'd go on TV—live —scene by scene.

As the show's opening music swelled throughout the studio, my whole body shook. My heart pounded and the adrenalin started flowing.

I finally had that chance to do plenty of crying scenes. I began to feel more and more like an actress. Carol had lots of things to cry about during those first few years on the show, and she's been crying ever since!

Two years later I had the feeling that my role wasn't going anywhere. Carol and her boy friend, Tom, looked like they were breaking up. But when I called the producer to ask if I was being written off the show, she said, "Oh no—we really love you. In fact, we have a story conference coming up and we'll find something new for you."

With her assurance, I relaxed and didn't think about it. But Carol seemed to be on the show less frequently, maybe once every two weeks or so. One day Carol was having a farewell scene, telling Tom goodbye as she was leaving to move to New York.

"There's no reason to stay here in Oakdale, Tom, so I might as well go to New York, unless you . . ."

"No, I think you're doing the right thing," Tom interrupted. "Take care of yourself."

There were tears in Carol's eyes when she heard his noncommittal reply.

At the time I didn't know that those tears would also be for me. A few days after Carol's goodbye scene, my agent called. I was sitting at the kitchen table when my mother picked up the phone. And I could sense by the way she spoke that something was wrong.

"You've been written off the show," she said softly.

I was stunned. "This can't be happening." Inside, I felt like a part of me had died. At nineteen, all I could think of was that I was losing my wonderful friends at "As the World Turns," friends who had become like a family to me. We had shared so much of each other's joys and sorrows, not only our problems on the set, but also our personal lives. And now I was leaving this family behind.

The producer tried to explain. She told me that they had tried to find a story angle, but that the writers didn't want Tom and Carol to marry yet. And the new writers thought my character was too in love with Tom to get involved with another man, so they dropped her. I knew from observation that things like this often happen on a soap opera. But it hurt too much to try to be realistic.

The day I cleared out my dressing room was dreadful. I looked longingly at the small dressing room I shared with Patsy Bruder, who plays Ellen, and Marie Masters, who is Susan, and I began to gather together my makeup, face cream, and tissues. Slowly, I took my shoes and extra robe out of my locker and closed the door for the last time.

The first person I met was the actor who played Tom. Our eyes met and we said our goodbyes. Then I saw Don Mac-

Laughlin, who played Tom's grandfather. He came up, put his arms around me, and gave me a big hug.

I thought, "I'm going to break any second." Fighting back tears, I hugged him tight. Because we had almost the same last name, people used to ask us if we were related. We would just smile, wink at each other, and say we were "kissin' cousins." Now he was telling me I'd go on to other things, and I was assuring him that I'd be okay.

But it wasn't easy. I was used to being introduced as "Rita McLaughlin, the girl who's on 'As the World Turns.'" I never realized how wonderful that was until people started to introduce me as the girl who "used to be on 'As the World Turns.'"

In the back of my mind I couldn't erase the thought that I had failed. "No matter what they had told me, if I had been good, they would have kept me." I thought that my career as an actress was over.

"Lord, if You don't want me to be an actress, tell me," I asked.

I had only been off "As the World Turns" for two months, but I thought that perhaps God had a different plan for me. I had always worked since I was eleven. And it was only because of my work that I had moved in the direction of being an actress. One job had led to another. I wouldn't have pursued acting at all if God hadn't opened the doors for me all along. Now, it seemed, the doors were closing. And I had a real sense that this was a turning point in my life.

"If this is a sign that You don't want me to work in show business, let me know."

A few months later God gave His answer. I auditioned for a part based on the comic strip "Mary Worth." It was for the role of a hippie, the exact opposite of the clean-cut girl-next-door type I'd played as Carol.

At the agency I was handed a six-page script. Scanning it quickly, I saw that I had a crying scene. So I went to the only place I could be alone to rehearse the script aloud and work on the emotion—the bathroom.

After I had waited about a half hour, it was my turn to audition. I had been able to cry in the bathroom, but would it happen again in front of the director? If I could make one moment in the scene real, I knew the director would be able to tell I could do the rest.

Well, I went through the scene with another actor and the tears came at the right spot. Inwardly, I was thanking God, knowing that the tears could just as easily not have come, when the director said something that I wasn't expecting. "You know, you are a great actress."

Driving home, I thought about the director's words. It seemed as though God were giving me His answer. And for the time being at least, it seemed to be His will that I keep at it.

I ended up taping the pilot for the program and the producers tried to sell it to the networks. But they were having trouble getting it on the air and I went up for other auditions.

Although ABC was seriously considering me for the part of Tara on a new soap opera, "All My Children," my heart still belonged to "As the World Turns." But it hurt too much to watch the show, and I lost track of the story. My mother, though, faithfully tuned in every afternoon, and one day she said excitedly, "I think they're bringing back Carol."

"Oh no," I thought. "If another girl plays the role, that'll be just awful."

A few weeks later I got the call I thought would never come. It was the producer. She said they had brought back the show's original writer, Irna Phillips, to help boost the ratings. And, it was true, they were also bringing back Carol and wanted me to play the part. What's more, they were planning a big storybook wedding—Carol's wedding—to Tom Hughes.

Although I was a junior in college, and right in the middle of exams, nothing mattered. I was back on "As the World Turns" and everything was perfect.

Preparing for the show was like getting ready for my own

wedding. The costume designer and I even selected the wedding gown from the showroom of Priscilla of Boston.

The wedding wasn't taped at the studio but at a beautiful church in Riverdale, New York. And I walked down the aisle surrounded by the cast and crew, who filled the church for the big event. Later, many of the soap opera magazines carried cover photos of "Carol and Tom's Wedding."

Now that I was back on the show, I had a dizzying schedule. I was taking a full load of courses at Marymount and planned that if I went to work during the day and to school at night I could graduate in June of 1973—the next year. But in order to manage this heavy load, I couldn't take the commuting from Brooklyn anymore. So I moved into a beautiful residence for women called St. Mary's, which was run by nuns. My room was long and narrow, with a magnificent floor-to-ceiling window at one end.

Before long, however, the hectic pace I was leading began to wear on me. I'd do a live show during the day, get home and take a few minutes to rest, whip up something to eat, do some schoolwork, then rush off to classes. By the time I got home at night I was dead tired. But I couldn't sleep yet. There were papers to type, books to read, scripts to memorize, dishes to clean, and clothes to wash. I never knew what to do first. And it felt like the room was closing in on me.

On top of that, I had the added emotion of the show. Carol was going through a lot of crying scenes, and even though her experiences were not mine, it still drained me to feel her misery and pour out her tears. It was as though I were going through traumatic experiences in my own life.

Because of the pressures, I did something I would deeply regret. I put aside the most important thing in the world to me —my relationship with God. We had always been so close and, without realizing it, I was taking His love for granted.

Every night before I did my homework, I'd resolve, "Tonight, I'm going to spend more time in prayer." But as I closed the last book, my eyelids also closed, and I found myself mum-

Our wedding. (Photo by Damon E. Dunn)

"I loved it—tap dancing, ballet—everything."

On the set of "Mr. Wizard" with Don Herbert.

Rita with Mitch Miller backstage at the NBC studios.

One of Rita's favorite portraits, taken by her father.

A performance shot from *A Phoenix Too Frequent* done in 1971. With Rita are Con Roche and Laura Taylor.

Rita with Pat Boone.

. . . with Oral Roberts.

bling, "Lord, I'd love to pray more, but You know how tired I am. I know You understand. Thanks for everything."

But one day the reassuring presence of God that I had always felt so strongly was gone. Added to the pressures of school and work was the strain of breaking up with my boy friend of two years. I felt confused, hurt, and broken. My head was spinning. With exams coming up and papers overdue, I reached the breaking point.

"Oh God, where are You?"

He seemed so far away, and I panicked.

I knelt down in the middle of my cluttered room and cried out to God, "Please take over my life. I'm nothing without You. I just can't do it. I want You more than I want anything in the world." I sat on the floor for a long time, just reaching out to God and not thinking about anything else.

It wasn't that God had ever left me. Instead, I had pushed Him out of the center of my life and had filled it up with everything else. I needed to get things back in order and put God first.

A strong desire to grow closer to Him grew in me and I looked for any way I could to feed my spiritual hunger. Sundays were a powerhouse. Besides going to church, I'd watch the TV shows of Oral Roberts, Rex Humbard, and Dr. Robert Schuller. I taped Billy Graham's crusades and would play them over again later. He sent me *The Living Bible*, and although I had read the Bible before, it really came alive for me with this modern paraphrase.

I was like a dry sponge absorbing everything that would draw me closer to God. It was wonderful to love Him and feel His powerful love in return. When pressures of school and work started to build, Christian music like *Pat Boone Sings the New Songs of the Jesus People* cleared my mind and lifted my spirit. June of '73 finally came. I graduated with a degree in communication arts and moved back home to Brooklyn.

The more I listened to my Christian records and TV shows,

the more I wanted to talk about God with others my age. I had heard about young people who were on fire for Jesus, and I asked God for a Christian friend.

"Please let me meet somebody who really loves You and believes Your Word," I prayed.

One day I happened to stop into Calvary Bookstore, which was across the street from the gym where I exercised almost every day. There I met Anita Chenoweth, who invited me to a Bible study. Though my friendship with Anita, I met other young Christians and came to understand the importance of Christian fellowship.

It was at a young Christian singles meeting at Calvary Baptist Church where I first heard a young woman give her personal testimony. I was amazed. Before a large group of people she was openly sharing what Jesus had done for her. I looked around the room and saw that each person was carrying a worn Bible. And they carried their Bibles around with them as though it were the most natural thing in the world.

I wanted to wear out my Bible too and memorize special verses that meant a lot to me.

And I wanted to learn more about what God had planned for me. In one of Pat Boone's books, *A New Song*, he mentioned how Christian businessman George Otis had led him into a fuller walk with God through the infilling of the Holy Spirit. To learn more, Anita and I attended some prayer meetings of the Full Gospel Business Men's Fellowship. It was made up of Christians from all denominations who gathered together to praise and worship God. They believed that the gifts of the Spirit—such as healing, prophecy, and speaking in tongues—were just as relevant today as they were in biblical times.

I attended many prayer meetings where everyone would spontaneously praise God. Often the songs and the overwhelming presence of God touched me so deeply that my eyes would fill up. Looking around, I'd see others, with handkerchiefs, not minding their tears of joy because they loved God so much.

I heard that George Otis was to be guest speaker at a banquet at the Americana Hotel in New York, so my mother and I bought tickets. There, a simple conversation with George before the meeting ultimately led to a turning point in my life.

He had been autographing books, and as I waited my turn, other people in line began asking for my autograph. When I finally met him, he asked me what I did and I told him about "As the World Turns."

Inside the Imperial Ballroom there were three thousand people sitting at tables of ten, filling the room to capacity. After some hymns and prayers, George was introduced and he stepped to the podium.

"Before I begin," he said, "I'd like to ask Rita McLaughlin, star of 'As the World Turns,' to come up here and share a few words with us."

"What?" I gasped. "He can't mean it." But he repeated his words and I knew I had to get up there.

"What could I possibly say to inspire these people?" I wondered, zigzagging my way through the tables as people whispered, "Oh, there's Carol" and "Hi, Carol."

I didn't have much time to think about what I would say. It was as if God simply threw me in the water and said, "Swim."

"God is the source of my life," I told them. "Especially doing a live show, I depend totally on God." I recounted some of my TV experiences and the tension of doing crying scenes and remembering lines. After a few more words, I thanked them and stepped down.

At that moment, a new sense of God's plan for my life was becoming clear to me. By thrusting me in front of those people at the Americana, God was answering the prayer I had had as a nine-year-old child, kneeling in my church in Brooklyn. At that time I had asked God to use me. He didn't want me to be a nun, I knew that. But I had desperately wanted to share the Gospel in some way. I always thought it would have been great to be a disciple at the time of Christ. But what I hadn't realized was that God could use me as His witness today—now—and specifically as an actress.

The very work God had given me would be the vehicle to tell people about Jesus. My being an actress had been God's plan all along!

I began to get more and more speaking invitations around New York. And whenever Christians knew that I was in town, they'd ask me to share my personal testimony—my experience with Christ. In Garden Grove, California, I was the guest on "Hour of Power" at the beautiful Garden Grove Community Church, and I spoke with evangelist Mario Murillo at Melodyland Christian Center. And in Florida I spoke before a Full Gospel meeting.

On one trip to California, I went to a Bible study at Pat Boone's home. There were about fifty actors and actresses there—people like Dean Jones, Chuck Woolery, and JoAnn Phlug. They were sitting on chairs and sprawled on the thickly carpeted floor. Pat came in after a singing engagement and led us in hymns. And then he said, "You know, in this profession we always hear the applause. But what greater thing could we do than give the applause to God?"

With that, everyone stood up and applauded.

God had been so good to me. I think that my applause must have been the loudest of all that night. I knew that God could use me as an actress.

Soon I would learn that I was not called alone.

4

NORMAN'S STORY

"The Making of a Minister"

For as long as I can remember, I wanted to be a minister. When I was very young, my mother gave me the idea to be a missionary doctor. But what I identified with most as a kid was the minister. When my father, who was Sunday School superintendent, stood in the pulpit, I'd think about how much I wanted to be there too.

One night when I was about five, some friends and I sneaked into the church after a covered-dish supper, and I climbed into the pulpit and pretended I was the pastor.

In spite of my wanting to be a preacher, however, it wasn't until I was about eight that my faith became my own. What finally led me to Christ was TV. I was all alone, watching Billy Graham give the invitation to accept Christ.

"Don't worry about the people you're with," he was saying. "They'll wait on you. Just come down and stand in front."

That night, the invitation was for me.

I went to my room and opened my Bible. There was no particular passage I had in mind; the decision was already made to give my life to the Lord.

The first person I told was my sister, who responded blankly, thinking that her younger brother was going through a phase.

By the time I reached junior high school, the fire in me seemed to fade. My priorities had shifted, and becoming a minister seemed far away. What was on my mind was girls and hanging around with the guys. I got a big kick out of swearing. I had a radio glued to my ear blaring rock 'n' roll, and a grease stick in my pocket to slick back my hair.

I was adrift. I'd still go to church on Sundays, but more out of obligation to my parents than anything else. And Sunday mornings were such a hassle.

In high school I was aimless and unmotivated and took the lazy way through school. I read *Life* magazines in the back of French class. If there was a test, I could remember just enough from class to pass. History was even better, because I could get by on essay tests with ideas off the top of my head. And I did get by—with C's and D's.

Afternoons I'd wear my jacket with my collar turned up and my hair slicked back, and hang out with the guys at Alphonso's pizzeria. It was great—doing nothing, thinking about nothing. I didn't have a care in the world. As for the future, I figured maybe I'd go to refrigeration school. But mostly I didn't worry about it.

Every now and then, though, a sermon would flash through my mind, reminding me of the dreams I had had as a kid. Buried beneath the "cool" front of the greasy hair, the seed of salvation was working in me. Norman may have opted for refrigeration school, but God had other plans.

It took a beach party to wake me up to the fact that I had been like the Prodigal Son in a faraway land. A buddy of mine who was in the youth group of the local Baptist church invited me to a Saturday beach party at Ocean Grove, New Jersey. It sounded all right—I never turned down a chance to meet girls.

"Why not?" I said.

The party was great. I liked a girl in the group, and at the end of the evening we all sat around the campfire singing hymns. Under the stars, with the logs of the campfire glowing, some kids gave their testimony, telling us how Jesus had given direction to their lives and how He had made them see that they had a purpose in school and in their relationships with others.

As I sat there listening to them share their problems and joys, I had to admit that the life they had was a whole lot happier than my life at Alphonso's pizzeria with the guys. And their words seemed to trigger memories of the little boy long ago who stood in the pulpit to preach.

I started going regularly to the youth group, and got closer and closer to my new group of Christian friends. At the same time, I was still hanging out with the guys, and for about a year I was caught between the world of the church and the world of my friends in school.

But at the end of my junior year in high school, my life began to change. The youth group elected me to be vice-president. It was the first time anyone had given a vote of confidence in my leadership abilities.

My life took on new purpose and a new zeal. I wanted to make that youth group the best ever, and so I began to make big plans for the coming year. When September rolled around, everything was different for me in school, too. It may sound unbelievable, but from grades of D's and F's, I started taking home A's and B's. My mother thought I was joking when I handed her my report card for the first semester.

As I did better in school, my goals shifted. For the first time I thought seriously about going to a liberal arts college. But in spite of my good showing my senior year, I still graduated in the bottom tenth of my class, because of my years of laziness.

What college would take me?

On the recommendation of our youth leader, I applied to Kings College in New York, and miraculously they accepted me—but only because my entrance exam scores were high.

And there was a condition: I was on probation and had one semester to get my grades high enough to prove I could succeed in college.

As it turned out, college was much harder than I expected. In high school I had always been able to get by even though I hadn't studied. Now, as a new college student, I seemed so far behind everyone else.

During freshman orientation my mind was spinning with new problems I had never confronted. I didn't even know how to fill out a schedule for classes, didn't know what courses to take, and was completely confused about the assignments my professors were giving me.

"I can't do this," I said to myself.

Frustrated, I climbed a big hill on campus to be alone, and found a beautiful, solitary spot overlooking the Hudson River.

I thought to myself, "I've got to leave. I know I'm going to flunk out, so why not quit while I'm ahead.

"God, you've got to help me."

As I lay back on the grass, watching the clouds pass silently overhead, the Lord very clearly brought to my mind something we had talked about in youth group. I remembered how God had helped Moses face the challenge of leading the Israelites.

"Lord, I'm not eloquent," Moses had said. "I am slow of speech and tongue." And God said to Moses, "Who has made man's mouth . . . Is it not I, the Lord? Now therefore go, and I will be with your mouth and teach you what you shall speak."

God was talking to me. He was telling me, as He had told Moses, "You're going to make it."

The Lord was so real at that moment that I could answer in my heart with confidence, "Yes, I am going to make it."

I smiled to myself as I walked back down the hill. I had learned an important lesson about Christian living. Here I was confused, living in a world I knew very little about, and I was smiling. God had refused to let me give up. It was as simple as that. This was the first time in my life that I had real problems, and it amazed me that God really did care about Norman Walter.

Then came those terrible Friday history quizzes. I'd stay up all night Thursday to prepare for those tests. It took a box of crackers and a whole jar of peanut butter to keep me awake. In high school I had never trained my mind to memorize, and now it was torture.

I took one quiz and got a B. But on the second quiz, I got a D. Then the teacher sent a shudder through my body.

"I grade my quizzes A, B, C, and Vietnam," he said. The rumors started flying that if you weren't in the top half of the class you'd be drafted.

The night before each exam I'd wake up in a cold sweat. I'd have a full-fledged anxiety attack. I'd bolt straight up in the middle of the bed, thinking, "I'm going to wind up in Vietnam."

But at the height of my anguish the Lord would quiet me down. I would remember that day on the hill, and I would hear Him say, "I told you that you're going to make it."

The fear would still come back, but each time it was less intense than before. And the voice of God grew stronger.

By midterm, though, the results still weren't in for my future. I failed my history and botony tests. "Lord, what's happening?" I asked. I wondered how I could face my parents and my friends. I was losing roommates left and right. One of my roommates flunked out at midterm and came back a few weeks later with his head shaved and wearing an Army uniform. At night I'd fall asleep with Army boots marching in my head.

Then I'd overhear kids who were on the verge of flunking out say with resignation, "I guess it's the Lord's will that I'm supposed to flunk out."

But I couldn't settle for that. "The Lord told me I'll make it," I reminded myself. "I can't say it's the Lord's will if I flunk out. If I do, it will be my own fault."

Slowly the quizzes and tests started turning around, with grades of C's and B's. Further down the line came the A's.

By the end of the semester, my grades were good enough to get me off probation. At last I was headed toward a college degree.

Although I considered myself studying for the ministry, college seemed to shake the roots out of everything. I didn't know where I was going to end up. Graduation was still a far-off goal that God had promised.

But as I began to grow more confident in my courses, I felt free to open up other areas of my life. So when I got an unexpected call from a friend, Pastor Brown, asking me to be temporary youth director at his church, I jumped at the chance. The church was in my home town—Jersey City—and the job was working with city kids who were tough on the outside but soft on the inside.

During my last two years of college I worked at the church. On Sundays I taught Sunday school, and sometimes Pastor Brown would let me preach at the service. In the afternoon I went to one of the local housing projects where I preached to a group of senior citizens in a big recreation hall they had turned into a "church." Later on were junior-high youth meetings, and in the evenings college and career groups. On Mondays I'd be back at school hitting the books.

I wondered if the day would ever come when I would actually be a pastor—full time. But that was too much to ask for. I had already told God that if He got me through college I'd never ask for another thing.

But God didn't give me a chance to wonder about my future for long. As graduation drew near, God was making it very clear that He was calling me to the ministry. People began to advise me to find a large church in the suburbs with a growing congregation that would assure me of a good future.

Then to everyone's surprise, Pastor Brown decided to leave his church, and the pulpit committee asked me to take over his job. I thanked them for their confidence and asked for time to pray about it. It was a small church, with no choir and a small membership, but I had grown to love it.

My parents invited me on a short vacation in Hawaii, and

while I was there I prayed about the situation. At the time, I kept thinking that maybe I could serve the Lord better in a bigger church with lots of well-organized programs and a senior pastor to guide me. And I thought, too, about an old friend who was pastor of a large church on Long Island. "If there's one person I'd like to work with, it's him."

Then a strange thing happened. As soon as I returned from Hawaii, he called to offer me a job as youth director of his church. It seemed like the perfect church and the perfect job. And the fact that he called seemed too coincidental.

"This must be where God wants me," I thought. I prepared to say goodbye to Jersey City.

But again, God had other plans. A devastating fire hit the recreation hall of the housing project in Jersey City where I preached to the senior citizens on Sunday afternoons. No one was hurt, but the arsonist had stolen our communion set.

In spite of the looting, in spite of the burning, we kept the services going in another building. I looked at the faces of those old people who were so grateful to hear the Word of God preached to them, no matter what the setting, and I thought, "*This* is where God wants me—I'm sure of it." He didn't want me in a big, affluent suburban church. He wanted me in the city that I loved, sharing the joys and problems that city people face.

"I'm sorry," I told my friend on Long Island. "The Lord has shown me that I belong here in Jersey City." I went back to the pulpit committee of Pastor Brown's church and told them I wanted to be their minister.

Sundays were the most fantastic days of all. I would get up, sit in my office and go over my message. And even when it was raining or cloudy, the sun seemed to stream in the window of my office.

In the little sanctuary, I looked up at the big stained-glass "Ascension" window.

"Lord, this is exactly where I want to be." As I walked into the empty pews, waiting for the congregation to arrive, I thought back on those long, tough college days. "Oh, Lord. I remember that day You told me You were going to pull me through college, and Your promise of a ministry.

"Truly, Lord, this is it. I couldn't be happier than I am at this moment."

As happy as I was in Jersey City, I knew I couldn't feel completely prepared for the ministry unless I was ordained. God had led me to be a full-time pastor rather than go to a seminary, but I knew that I needed the credentials of ordination.

So I went to my home pastor, a man with two seminary degrees who was serving an independent Baptist church that in the past had ordained only top men. And I told him that I had a call to the ministry.

"If you'd be willing to study for an examination, I'd be willing to sponsor you for ordination," he said. "But it isn't going to be easy."

His church licensed me as a lay pastor, and for the next seven months I studied to prepare for a rigorous oral exam. By the time the exam came, I thought I was ready for anything.

Sixteen ministers faced me on the ordination council. At first their questions and my answers seemed to go along without problems. I described my salvation experience in front of the TV during the Billy Graham Crusade, presented the doctrinal statement I had prepared, and then described the miraculous way God called me to the Jersey City church through the blaze in the housing project.

For the next two hours their questions probed every possible area of the ministry. I knew that God was with me, because as they asked difficult doctrinal questions the answers came to me complete with Bible verses to back them up. This was the college student who couldn't memorize!

The panel seemed to respond warmly and positively. My pastor nodded in approval and a big smile spread over his face.

But then, one of the panelists leaned forward and asked, "What would you do if you discovered that one of your Sunday school teachers smoked?"

I knew that he expected me to say that I'd ask him to step

down from his job. But I also knew that one of the most devoted Christians in my congregation—a deacon—smoked.

"I wouldn't encourage it," I said, "but I wouldn't ask him to leave on that basis alone. His Christian commitment would be the most important thing."

As I expected, the answer was not well received by the council. The smile left my pastor's face. Then they hit me with another question that headed us toward a collision course. "Would you allow the speaking of tongues in your church?"

My heart sank. Although I didn't have any members of my congregation who spoke in tongues, I had gotten to know several ministers in Jersey City who did. Watching them work, and hearing them share the close experience they had with Christ, convinced me that deep down these were men of God, no matter what their form of worship or label.

"The Bible says, 'Do not forbid speaking in tongues,'" I answered. "And I believe that all of the miracles described in the Bible could happen today as well as at the time of the early church."

Now my pastor's head was buried in his arms. I couldn't tell if he was feeling my pain with me or was deeply disappointed in me.

I left the room with a heavy heart, knowing that I could not compromise what I believed, even if it meant being denied the ordination I wanted so desperately. I didn't know it then, but the answers that I gave would soon take on even greater personal meaning for me. And my ordination was just the first step of an even bigger test that God would put me through, as He shaped me as a minister and as a husband.

About a half hour later, my pastor asked me to come back into the room. The faces were serious. The chairman of the council stood up and said, "Norman, we have decided to approve your ordination. But we are recommending that you meet with your pastor several times to discuss these matters."

I walked away from the council as Rev. Norman Walter, an ordained minister of the Baptist Church.

Life in my Jersey City church was swirling with activities. There was the youth group to run, people to visit in the hospital, baptisms and marriages to perform. It was a twenty-four-hour-a-day job, and I loved it.

I think the best times with my youth group came at Christmas. Most of the young people were street-wise city kids who were very different from the youth groups I had known in high school. But at Christmas the face of the whole city changed. Drab houses and stores became little holiday show-places. At our youth meeting we would decorate a tree, turn down the lights, and then share the timeless story of God's love in a manger in Bethlehem. Even today I remember the warmth that came over their faces as we sang the carols.

And I especially loved the old people—those marvelous senior citizens in their makeshift church in the housing project which I visited on Sunday afternoons. On top of that, I was asked to take over the preaching in a nursing home.

Every Tuesday I'd drive to the home and share a message with the sixty to seventy people who came regularly. Most came in their wheelchairs; others walked to the services assisted by nurses or using canes. Some were too sick to come at all, and after the service I'd try to stop by and visit with each one for a while.

Along with the nursing home ministry, at the mayor's request, I got involved in a drug rehabilitation program for teen-agers. And through this work I came in contact with many priests and nuns in our area who were dedicated to the same urban mission that I was and who shared my faith in Christ.

My ministry was expanding, and I was growing through the experience of meeting new Christians from different backgrounds and new challenges. But there was one glaring weakness in my ability to cope with these challenges, and it became increasingly, and painfully, clear to me as the weeks went on. I suffered from a severe case of stage fright. I was afraid to stand up in front of people and talk, and it was months before

I felt comfortable speaking before my little congregation and at the nursing home. But whenever I was called on to speak elsewhere, I lost all confidence—my heart would pound, my voice would quiver, and my face would sweat.

I knew that the only way to overcome this fear was to keep preaching, wherever and whenever I could. So I went to a friend who was a pastor and said, "I'd like to volunteer to speak to some groups for you. Give me anybody, and I'll do it."

"Sure," he said. "In fact, there's something you can help me with right now. Could you take my radio show for me?"

"You mean, be a guest on your show?" I asked.

"No, I need someone to take the whole show."

"When is it?" I asked.

"This Sunday."

I was on the spot. This was the first thing he had asked me to do and I couldn't say no. So I prayed. Hard. And on the appointed day I nervously drove to the studio for the half-hour show. It was live, on the "Pillar of Fire" network WAWZ, and it reached thousands of people in the New Jersey area.

The show's format sounded simple enough. I was supposed to give a message and answer phone calls of prayer requests. Only a few minutes after I had launched into my message and paused for a minute, the engineer signaled to me through the glass booth that someone was on the line with a prayer request.

Right there—in the middle of my message—I had to stop and offer a prayer. I almost panicked, trying to remember where I had left off. But somehow God helped me find my place, and before long the engineer was back with another prayer request.

One long half hour later I wound up with a prayer and went off the air. And I just sat there quietly, thinking about what had happened. I was afraid to speak before groups, and I had just managed to speak to thousands of people without fainting.

"Thank You, Lord."

The engineer signaled to me again: "There's a call for you from the station manager."

I thought, "I hope I didn't do anything wrong."

The first words out of the station manager's mouth were, "Would you take a regular program?" That was the beginning of a radio ministry that continued through my years in Jersey City and to this day.

As for the stage fright, it stayed with me. But as I continued to speak to various small groups, God helped me to keep speaking even though my knees shook and my heart thumped.

One of the most difficult lessons I had to learn was that all things in this life, even the most precious to us, someday come to an end. After five wonderful years in Jersey City, God said, "It's time to move on." Ironically He led me to a well-established surburban church. This opportunity was a real promotion, and I thanked God for it. But leaving my home and church family was the hardest thing I ever had to do. The Jersey City church had grown and we now had a choir and a stable budget. We had all become more a part of each other's lives than we realized, and my last weeks in the city were filled with smiles and tears and embraces. But what made the parting a little easier was the knowledge that my father, who as a lay preacher had often substituted for me in the pulpit, had now been licensed by the church to be their pastor.

I reassured the congregation that they would continue to grow and that things would be better than ever. But inside I knew that a page had turned in all of our lives.

Now a beautiful TV star, Rita McLaughlin, had just walked into my life.

She was standing beside me now on our first date—it was like an incredible dream. I had just kissed her, and I was on top of the world.

5

"Spiritual Summit Conference"

His kiss was the most romantic in the world, so soft and gentle. The evening had ended too quickly and we had to say good night. Since my mother was staying overnight, she had kept the keys to the apartment. Norman and I never realized we'd be getting in so late, and I hated to ring the doorbell and wake her up. But after a minute or two the door opened.

"Why don't you invite him in for a minute?" she said to me, and went back to bed.

Norman and I walked over to the picture windows, and the whole city seemed to be lit up with sparkling, diamond lights. We stood there, arms around each other, looking out and not saying a word.

"You're *so* nice, Carol," Norman said. A few seconds later, he realized his mistake, and to put him at ease I came back with, "Thank you, Herman." And we both laughed.

A little while later, as Norman was leaving, he said, "So many times, when people have a nice time on a first date, it's never quite right on the second date. Let's always keep it the same as tonight."

After he left, I sat in the darkness, wondering what it all meant.

"It's true," I thought. "The magic is often gone on the second date. But somehow, this seems different."

Something had seemed different from the moment Norman had called to ask me out. I had just gotten home from work, and my mother said that he had called.

"Do you have the number? I'll call him back," I said.

There was a strange hesitation in her voice, and an even more curious question that seemed to suggest that somehow she knew this guy was special. "Are you sure you want to do that?" she asked. "After all, he *is* a minister."

"Sure, why not?" I answered.

"I'll tell you, his voice sounded really good," she said. "You'd better think twice before you call him."

As I ran upstairs to make the call, I reassured her, "Mom, it's only one date. That doesn't mean I'm going to marry him."

I called Norman from my room, and when he answered I was mesmerized by the sound of his voice. It was soft, peaceful, soothing. He offered to pick me up in Brooklyn for our date, but I insisted that I meet him in New York, where I would be staying for the next few weeks. I was apartment-sitting for Kathy Hays, who plays Kim on the show, and I hated to have Norman drive all the way to Brooklyn. I wanted everything to be special for him.

When I came through the lobby door of Kathy's apartment building, followed by my mother and brothers, I looked around to find someone who resembled a young Billy Graham —that's the way Steve and Terrie had described him. Across the lobby was a tall, sandy-haired man looking at me and smiling. Their description was perfect. It had to be Norman.

We were all alone in the elevator, and in the quietness of the moment I smiled to myself. "Wow, he's really something." I didn't know where it was going, but so far, so good.

There's always a certain awkwardness on first dates, but

Norman had a kindness and warmth that immediately put me at ease. As he sat at the dining room table, with sunlight surrounding him, I was struck by his strong, charismatic presence. I excused myself and went into the bedroom to check everything out in a mirror, and found my brother David there.

"Isn't he great?" I whispered to him.

He gave me a puzzled, younger-brother look and said, "I don't know; he's okay I guess."

But to me, this guy was special. On the way to the Lamb's Club, I felt like staying alone with him all night, just talking. I wanted to know all about him.

I knew he was my kind of guy when he accidentally dipped his tie into the salad dressing. That's just the kind of thing I might have done! He made me feel right at home.

There was something about Norman that was so mature, so together. He wasn't trying to impress anyone or put on an act. He was just straightforward and natural.

When it came time for the play, I was frustrated having to sit in my seat staring straight ahead. I wanted to know more about this person next to me. I was so fascinated by everything he said, and I respected his position as a minister so much. To think that he played such an important role in people's hearing about salvation. I wanted to get closer to him, but he seemed to be content watching the play.

We got the chance to be alone as we walked along Central Park after midnight. It was getting chilly, and my hands were cold. But then I felt him reach out, and his large, warm hand clasped mine. A warmth flowed through me, and my knees got weak.

I always hoped that someday I'd meet a nice Christian guy. But to find one who was also gorgeous and who had the right chemistry with just the touch of a hand—it was fantastic.

And then he kissed me so tenderly, so lovingly, at the apartment door. There was no doubt about it. Norman was different from the others.

Three days later he called, and there was the same warm

voice, the same confident, powerful presence that had attracted me on our first date. We arranged to meet the next day, Wednesday, at a studio where I was auditioning for a narration for a film.

My audition had just finished at eleven-thirty when a secretary said, "You've got someone waiting for you."

I was looking forward to seeing Norman again. The first date had been wonderful, but I knew that by the second date I'd know more about the kind of person he was.

We immediately found lots to talk about as we made our way out of the huge gray building. The weather was sunny and warm as we walked along Fifth Avenue past Tiffany's and Bergdorf Goodman. We agreed that this was a perfect day for a walk through Central Park. It was late July, and the park was fresh and green and full of the sounds of summer. This was a day to share with someone special.

The sunlight was shining on his hair, and those blue eyes . . . I couldn't stop looking at him. And inside I wanted so much to have everything go right that day. As we sat there, a middle-aged woman came up to us with a big smile on her face.

"I watch you on the show all the time," she said, "and I just have to shake your hand." I introduced Norman to her, gave her my autograph, and talked for a while.

Soon after she left, our conversation turned to the Bible, and we started talking about our favorite verses.

"My favorite is in the Old Testament," said Norman. "I've used it a lot for sending missionaries out, because it relates to giving your riches to others. But it's not that well known. It's Nehemiah 8:10."

"Oh," I said. "'For the joy of the Lord is your strength.'"

"That's it!" said Norman. "'Go your way, eat the fat, and drink the sweet, and send portions unto them for whom nothing is prepared: for this day is holy unto our Lord: Neither be ye sorry; for the joy of the Lord is your strength'" (King James).

Norman had picked one of the few Scripture verses in the Old Testament that I had memorized.

I thought, "Thank You, God." I remembered how I had read that verse in a daily blessing book that Oral Roberts had sent out. Each day I read a verse and a prayer, and I always tried to memorize the verse.

As we approached the lake in the middle of the park, we saw a few people in boats and some sitting on the grass nearby. The smell of french fries and hamburgers drifted from the boathouse with its green roof glistening in the sun. As we walked along the water we talked about our first date and laughed about some of the apprehensions we had had about each other before we met. We seemed to cover everything—our work, our families, and all the things most important to us.

Together we crossed continents that afternoon, miles and miles of thoughts and ideas.

The questions we asked each other were much more personal than those you would ordinarily ask someone on a second date. We both loved the Lord so much and He was first in our lives. As a result, it became clear to us that we didn't want to get involved in a relationship that would jeopardize our faith in any way. So we had to ask questions—serious questions. We needed to know much more about each other before we let the relationship grow.

As we sat there in the park, we had a feeling that was building so quickly for each other. At one point, we laughed because he had called me Carol instead of Rita on our first date. And then he said softly, "I'm looking forward to the time when I can call you something more personal than Rita." And then we began to explore our deep feelings about our faith.

I wondered, "Is everything I believe going to contradict what he believes?"

As a minister and a Christian, of course, he was particularly concerned about my beliefs. I enjoyed the questions—about communion, about confession, and most of all about explaining my position. I had been around a lot of Protestants and felt comfortable talking with them. Not only had I met many devoted Christians who were Protestants, I had also seen the ecumenical movement grow in the Catholic Church. I regarded Protestants and Catholics as brothers in Christ. We were both following Jesus—that was what was important.

Although I'm no theologian, in my own way I could explain what I believed. My biggest concern as I talked with Norman was to clear up whatever false ideas he might have had about the Catholic Church—misconceptions I had heard over and over again.

Typical was confession.

"Do you really believe you have to confess your sins to somebody else?" Norman asked, picturing in his mind the priest sitting in a confessional and a parishioner coming before him to confess and be forgiven.

"First of all," I told him, "it used to be traditional for Catholics to go to confession before they could take communion. But then the Church felt that the people had gotten the wrong attitude. Some thought they had to be cleansed in confession before they could receive communion. Instead, the Church stressed a personal act of contrition, asking God to forgive us. Then we could come to communion as sinners, redeemed in Christ.

"The Bible says, 'Confess your sins to one another.'" Then I added, "God forgives you outside of confession as well. But confession is simply an outward sign of God's forgiveness."

Norman listened patiently, but the expression on his face was one of concern. "But the Bible says there is one mediator between God and man, Christ Jesus," said Norman.

"I believe our sins are forgiven because Christ died on the cross," I said. "Whether I confess my sins to a priest, to a person I might have hurt, or to you, Norman, what's important is that I want to have my sins forgiven and make amends. The priest shows God's love and forgiveness and often counsels when someone needs it."

"Well," he said, "I see your point, as long as you recognize that it's God who has the power to forgive sin. The priest is a listener and I can see where it helps to have a trained Christian counselor there to guide you. In fact, I try to encourage my congregation to be more open with me about their own problems with sin. But the important thing to realize is that there is no replacement for personal communication with the Lord in prayer. That's what knowing Christ personally is."

I agreed.

Then there was the issue of baptism. As we talked, though, it became clear that what was important to both of us wasn't the form of baptism but the reality of following Christ and the Bible. I had been baptized as a child, but I knew that that in itself wasn't enough to ensure that I was right with God.

"I know one thing," I told Norman. "Unless a person has made a personal commitment to Christ, baptism won't help him or her get into heaven. When I look in the Bible, I see the emphasis on a personal relationship with Christ, not on infant baptism."

To us, our discussion that day was as important as any summit conference of world leaders. Our differences were obvious, but these very differences made finding common ground even more rewarding. Our common ground, however we phrased it, was consistently the Bible.

You see, we both believe that the Bible is the perfect Word and authority of God, so the issues that divided us began to seem smaller and smaller. What became obvious was that we both had the same faith. Again and again our expressions of concern became smiles of agreement. But more than that, I began to realize that this was the person I had been praying for, the kind of man I wanted to share my whole life with. A sensitive, loving man but one with deep, unmoving faith. Anyone in his right mind would have told me it was too soon to know this. But I knew.

Later that evening, as we talked over dinner, I was struck by the deep love that I was feeling for him. Our conversation was light and happy compared to the deep discussion of the afternoon. We laughed so much that night. It wasn't a forced or social laugh. It was the kind of laughter that you just can't hold in.

For a moment, everyone and everything in the world faded away except for the two of us. Now Norman's face was serious, but the faintest smile lingered as he looked deeply into my eyes.

"You know, this might sound strange, but . . ."

"What is it?" I asked.

"Well, I know we've only had two dates . . . But I know everything I need to know that I love you . . . and that I want to marry you."

I had rehearsed a lifetime for this moment. I'd always wondered if I'd be nervous or tongue-tied.

Instead, I looked at him and said quietly, "Ask me."

"Rita, will you be my wife?"

My mind was way ahead of him. I started talking about how many children we would have.

"Well, will you marry me?" he asked again.

"Oh, we'll get married," I said. "I just want to know if you'd like a big family or not."

When I got home, the whole thing hit me. Here it was, our second date, and I had accepted his marriage proposal. Norman was the most wonderful man I had ever met. He was kind and caring and fun to be with. He had a deep love of God and was a moral person. But he was also a Baptist minister. It frightened me to think of our different backgrounds, and I wondered if we were doing the right thing.

I had dinner with a friend, Sister Margaret, who led a weekly prayer group. I respected her spiritual advice and explained the difficult situation to her. "What do you think about this?" I asked her. "After all, he's a Baptist minister . . . I guess you think I'm not right for him and should break it off."

Sister Margaret looked at me lovingly. She knew I wanted God's will and was struggling with a decision. "Who do you think you are?" she asked. "Put it in God's hands. If He wants the two of you together, He'll work it out. He'll close the door if it's not right."

I was surprised by her answer and encouraged by her faith. I knew I had to trust God with my relationship with Norman, and that's what I wanted more than anything else. When we saw each other Friday night for our third date, all I could think of was how much I wanted to be with him for the rest of my life.

Saturday morning we talked on the phone about the problems ahead. And Norman was reassuring. "We can find unity in Christ. That's the answer for us."

But later that day when I talked with my mother, she expressed concerns that I had hoped could be worked out. "Look, Rita," she said. "You're an actress and he's a minister. How can it work out? Besides, as a Catholic, no matter how much you two share, how can you really help his ministry?"

My mind was spinning. I wanted him so much, and yet I didn't want to hurt him in any way. Those thoughts began to nag at me, and by the afternoon I knew what I had to do. I sat in my room, waiting for Norman to call. I was overcome by the problem of having to end our relationship.

The phone rang and it was Norman. A few minutes into the call, I said what I felt I had to say. "I'm no good for you, Norman. There's a girl out there somewhere for you—a nice Protestant girl whom everybody would accept, and she would complement you in every way. There are just too many differences between us. And I think maybe it would be better for you . . . if we stopped seeing each other."

I choked on the words and couldn't say anymore. I felt so strongly about him. I didn't want to call it love so soon, but I knew that's what it was. And yet, here I was, telling him it was over.

There was silence on the other end. Then, trying to sound calm, Norman said, "Well . . . if that's the way you feel, but I've been thinking about it, too, and I think we can work it out. We've got so much going for us. Don't run away from the problem. Let's face up to it and deal with it. We can do it. With God behind us, we can do it. I know we can."

His words quieted my fears, and I loved him for it.

"Do you really think we can?" I asked, beginning to get hopeful.

"We can work it out, Rita," Norman said. As he talked, I began to see that we had time, and that with time perhaps there could be unity and that we could be together.

When the call ended, I heard Norman saying softly, "Goodbye, Rita. I love you." As I hung up the phone, I suddenly felt devastated by everything. I had almost lost him and felt such a tremendous release that all I could do was cry.

Later that night I wrote in my diary, "We saw each other last night on our 'bong' third date. There's no guy I could talk to and admire and respect so much. It's crazy for the third date, but I really love that pastor.

"Problems now arise about Catholic-Protestant. He called this morning and we talked about unity. It just hit me what kind of a relationship we could have eventually, united by faith, and it really shook me up. I feel calmer now, but I'd even told him when he called back this afternoon that maybe we should split.

"But how could I ever leave him? I would, Lord, if it were Your will. It was a little rough on him, and on me, of course. It showed an immaturity in me—a desire to run away from the problem. But I just want to do whatever is right, even if it means not seeing him.

"Norm says I'm jumping the gun, making the problem worse than it needs to be. He said that I should let our relationship grow, let the Lord work, and communicate and not just throw the whole thing down the drain. I guess I was over-reacting because I was tired.

"You know, Lord, I don't know what's going to happen to me and Norm. But right now I've got to admit I feel such a love, a deep love, a holy love. You can't not love a pastor with a personality like his. (Not to mention the fact that he thinks

I'm kind of okay too.) He says his parents want to meet me. His mom's a fan.

"Oh God, Norm and I seem so right. But if it isn't of You, and we pray to You often, let us know. Please let us know soon. It would be awful to hang on to a relationship that wasn't Your will.

"I guess I have to keep loose, be open and pray to the Lord and let God talk to me. I just want God's will to be done. I know, Lord Jesus, that You are going to make it clear to us in the coming weeks, and for that I'm grateful.

"Frances Hunter prayed I'd meet a guy soon who'd just pick me like a rose in a garden. I hope I've found my picker. Thank You, Jesus. Open the way for me to see the light. Praise You, Lord. I love You so much."

As I wrote in the diary that night, I was conscious of one thing. I loved Norman, but more than anything else, I wanted to do God's will, even if it meant giving him up.

6

NORMAN'S STORY

"Courtship with Christ"

I couldn't believe what I was hearing on the phone. Rita and I had shared three wonderful dates. We had discussed everything and had uncovered some differences. But we knew it could work. Now Rita was telling me that the differences were too great.

"We can make it. With God behind us, we can do it. I know we can."

"Norman . . . I'm sorry, but I really believe it's best for you if we stop seeing each other."

Our voices were both close to tears as I made one more effort to change her mind. Then I told her I loved her and hung up. Everything in her voice told me it was over.

Later that day I was invited to join a group of young marrieds from my church for a picnic at Greenwood Lake. My spirits were as low as they could go, but I knew I couldn't just sit and think. One of the husbands said, "Come on, Pastor, we're going to take a spin in the motorboat."

When we got to the middle of the lake, the engine died. Naturally we had no oars on board, so all we could do was yell to the wives onshore. Everyone else was in stitches, but I thought I had reached the end of the line.

All I could hear was the lapping of the water on the boat. I was lost in my thoughts, rehashing my conversation with Rita, and thinking about what the future would be like without her.

Later that night, I went to a young-adult party at our church and things were even worse. It was a beautiful midsummer's night, the kind of night that makes you glad to be alive and to have someone to love. I could hear the laughter and the music around me, but nothing penetrated my soul.

I thought, "We can't just leave it like this," and I made a decision to call her the next day. The next morning I braced myself to defend our love against any doubt. We could make it, I knew it.

But when Rita answered the phone, her voice was surprisingly fresh and open. This time she was saying what I had been saying, "I guess we can work it out. The problems aren't as great as they seem, especially since we both have Christ."

Overnight our relationship had gone from rags to riches, and we were together again. But just so she would know exactly how I felt about our love, I told her, "Rita, our love is so right and so obviously from God, that I'd give up everything for you." Those words were to take on a deeper meaning even sooner than I realized.

"I'm not asking you to do that," she said. "I'd never ask you to do that."

The rest of the conversation was light and cheerful. I told her about my day at the retreat, and now I could even laugh about the fact that the men had gotten stranded in the lake and had to be rescued by the women. As I started telling her about the party the night before, I found myself almost enjoying it in retrospect, because she was sharing it with me. This time, when we said goodbye, I knew it was not the end but only a momentary parting.

When we came together again, our relationship flooded

back like beautiful warm water. All of the wonderful memories of our first few dates, our talks, and our closeness took over. Together we started making plans for tomorrow, for next week, and for the rest of our lives.

The next few weeks were a whirlwind. We went to the studio, to restaurants for long talks, and to my church. Quickly I became part of her world, and she became part of mine.

My first visit to the studio gave me an exciting introduction to Rita's world. The studio was gigantic, and once I walked past the guards I entered a labyrinth of dressing rooms, with stages hidden behind big metal doors. I was wondering where to find Rita in this maze, when I saw a very familiar face. It was Larry Bryggman, who plays Dr. John Dixon in "As the World Turns." I had seen him in the show, and now for the first time I was seeing him face to face.

I introduced myself and asked him if he could show me to Rita's dressing room. He stopped what he was doing and stayed with me until we located Rita. Soon we ran into Don Hastings and Kathy Hays, who were as warm and friendly as I had imagined they would be. They all welcomed me as a friend, because I was special to someone very dear to them.

One afternoon I waited for Rita in the lobby of Archbishop Fulton J. Sheen's apartment building, where she had gone for a visit. She knew the Archbishop from the actors' retreats he had given at the Shubert Theatre during Lent. He had even helped her audition for the part of a nun on "The Bionic Woman" by giving her a quick emergency lesson in Latin pronunciation on the telephone when she called from a Hollywood audition.

When Rita told him about our love for each other and for Jesus, he gave her one of his books, *Life of Christ*. It was inscribed, "To Rita and Norman, with the blessings of Archbishop Sheen."

Rita willingly threw herself into my world, too, and was lovingly welcomed by my friends and congregation. On Sundays I picked her up at her home in Brooklyn and drove her to New Jersey just in time for my 11 A.M. service. Within minutes of her arrival the first Sunday, people recognized her and crowded around to shake her hand and hug her. Steve came over to me to find out how things were going. Just as he walked up, Rita turned to me and said, "Where do you want me to sit, honey?"

Steve looked surprised at our intimacy after only a week.

"Things are going well," I explained.

"Yeah, I picked that up," he said with a knowing smile.

The next week I announced that Rita would be taking the evening service. That night the congregation was swelled to overflowing with people, young and old, who had come to hear her speak. I had never seen so many people at one of our evening services before, and many were new to our congregation.

Rita took a hand mike, and instead of standing in the pulpit she walked to the floor of the sanctuary to be closer to the people.

"I just want to tell you tonight that I love Jesus and He's Lord of my life. I thank God that He made me an actress, but it's a far greater joy to be a Christian."

I was sitting on the platform behind her, so I could see the smiles on the faces of the congregation. Some may have thought that a Christian actress would either be "high and mighty" or "holier than thou." Instead, they found Rita to be a friend—a sister in the Lord.

"As a Christian I have many opportunities to share God's love on the set. God has also given me the privilege of speaking at many churches and crusades. People come out to meet the girl on their soap opera and many meet the Savior as well."

She then shared some actual experiences of witnessing for Jesus in her work. The congregation had been hanging on every word as she revealed a side of her that can't be communicated on a TV screen. It was the behind-the-scenes Rita I had fallen in love with.

That night the congregation fell in love with her too. At the end of the service she was surrounded by well-wishers, who told her how much she meant to them. "You don't know what a blessing you are to us," said one woman. "I always knew you were a Christian from watching you on TV."

Rita's faith and the love that flowed from her were teaching me something about Christianity as well. Whatever problems I might have had with the differences in our Christian backgrounds dissolved when I watched her share love with others. She was a living testimony to faith in action—patient, open, generous, humble, and loving. I could see it in the way she related to the young people in my church. She loved being with the kids, and somehow she had taken the time to learn each of their names. I could see her faith in the way she worked with the elderly in the nursing home where I ministered. As we went from room to room, visiting those who were too sick to come to the afternoon service, she would talk quietly to them one by one, making each one feel like the most important person in the world.

In everything she did, I could see Christ living in her. And patiently she helped open my eyes to the born-again Christianity in the Roman Catholic Church.

One Wednesday afternoon we visited a Bible study at St. Patrick's Cathedral. I had always loved St. Patrick's, and very often, before I met Rita, I would go there to pray. In the stillness of that great cathedral I always felt very close to God.

But now Rita was showing me a different side of St. Patrick's. She led me to a basement room that was filled with people who had come for the Bible study on their lunch hour. There were men in business suits, women with lunch bags. The study was led by a layman, and during the hour the people would share openly how God had helped them get through difficult times. There were no stained-glass windows —not even a priest—just a group of people sharing their faith in Christ.

I was deeply moved by their spontaneity, as they stood one after another to share Scripture verses they had come upon in their devotions.

"Wow," I thought, "there are people in the Catholic Church who have really had an experience with Christ. But then again, I've seen a lot of Catholics who haven't."

Then I realized what I was doing. I was assuming that if you weren't Protestant you didn't know Jesus as Savior. And there are plenty of Protestants who haven't had this kind of experience with Jesus.

It was ironic. During the past few weeks before meeting Rita, I had been preaching sermons about how we should be open to other Christians; how we shouldn't label people. I had been trying to counter some of the anti-Catholic tendencies in my own church.

And now, here with Rita, I was coming face to face with my own sermons. God was putting me to the test, asking me to put my faith where my mouth was.

I loved Rita so much, and I had been searching so long for the right Christian girl. All of a sudden, she was here. We dreamed the same dreams, and our inner spirits soared together.

When we were together, Rita and I prayed often that our faith would grow as our love was growing. We'd pray anywhere, in the car on the way to a picnic in the country, in her living room, in my parsonage.

"We're searching for the same thing, Lord," we prayed. "We're not a Baptist first, nor a Catholic first. We want to be Christians first. We want to be followers of Christ. Help us to focus on You, and then we will be one, in You."

The more we talked and prayed, the more our faith centered on Christ and on the Bible as a witness of His life. We stuck as close to the Bible as we could in formulating our faith position. If something was in the Bible, we hung on to it. If it wasn't, we decided it wasn't an issue we needed to resolve.

One day as we were driving in the country, I mentioned to Rita something that had been on my mind.

"Have you ever thought about being baptized?" I asked.

She looked surprised, but then she seemed to turn the idea

over in her mind. "What would it mean in relation to me? I mean, I was baptized as an infant and I'm already a Christian."

"The method of baptism isn't as important as what it signifies," I told her. "The Bible says that it means we have been crucified with Christ and risen to a new life with Him. Basically, baptism is a sign of what has already happened in your life, the same as communion symbolizes that we have already partaken of Christ's body and blood through faith. Just as Jesus was baptized by water, you can also experience baptism in the same way He did."

She thought a while longer. "I like the idea of being baptized now that I'm older and can experience what's happening. I've seen baptisms by immersion and they really did symbolize our death to sin and resurrection to new life in Christ. Where would it happen?" she asked.

"How about my first church in Jersey City?" I said. I knew that baptism is not a secret act but that it shouldn't be an exhibition, either.

"I think I'd like that," she said, smiling softly.

A few days later, we were in the car again, heading for my great old church in Jersey City, where Rita would be baptized. It had only been three weeks since we had met, and yet it seemed like we had lived through an eternity of togetherness. We were that close.

Rita's friend Marsha Clark was in the car too. She would be the only witness to the service. We planned to have the baptism by 2 P.M. in order to get Marsha back to the city for a 7:30 P.M. performance of a play she was appearing in.

But the best laid plans go awry, and we got in the middle of a traffic jam. What's more, the car causing the tie-up belonged to George Hansen, the Sunday School superintendent of my old church. We pulled over to the side of the road to help, and as we were about to leave George to find a tow truck, I looked in my rearview mirror and watched as a car slammed into the back of George's car. I ran back and opened the door. His glasses had been knocked off by the impact, and he was sitting frozen in the front seat.

A few minutes later, we found ourselves racing him to the emergency room of the local hospital. He had some bruises and a few broken ribs, so we stayed at the hospital until we were sure he was in good hands. Soon we were back on the way to the baptism.

The little church looked very special for this holy occasion. Sunlight was streaming through the stained-glass windows, filling the room with rainbow rays. Even the turn-of-the-century baptismal pool at the front of the church looked strangely beautiful. There was a leak at the top of the pool so I could fill it up only part of the way. But that didn't matter.

What mattered was this moment—this ordinance of Christ I was about to perform—and the feeling of love I felt for Rita. I put on my hip boots and black robe and went to check on Rita.

"You can come in," she said.

As I peered through the door of the waiting room to see if she was ready, my heart seemed to stop. She was sitting solemnly in a long white robe with the Bible open on her lap. Her red hair was hidden by a white bathing cap, and her glasses were perched on the edge of her nose as she pored over her Bible in prayer.

She had never looked more beautiful.

I took her hand and led her out into the church. The only sounds were the sloshing noises we made as we stepped into the warm water in the baptismal pool. Because the water level was so low, we knelt down. Marsha was standing before us. I began the service, reading from Romans 6.

"'Do you not know that all of us who have been baptized into Christ Jesus were baptized into His death? We were buried therefore with Him by baptism unto death, so that as Christ was raised from the dead by the glory of the Father, we too might walk in newness of life.'"

I said a short prayer and was about to continue with the service, when Rita said, "Can I read this?" She picked up the chapter where I had left off, and slowly repeated each word in order to prolong the cherished moment. "'For if we have been united with Him in a death like His, we shall certainly be united with Him in a resurrection like His'" (Romans 6:5).

When she finished, she looked up at me lovingly and said, "I'm going to pray, okay?"

"Of course, sweetheart," I said. She raised her hands in the air and said, "Oh God, thank You so much for Your love, for sending Your Son, Jesus, to die on the Cross for our sins, so that the price has been paid and we are free to live in the newness of life. I love You so much. Help me to live the way I should—doing only Your will and being a witness to others of Your tremendous love. Thank You for everything. You're the greatest. In Jesus' name, Amen."

Her fresh, innocent beauty in that white robe and bathing cap, and the simplicity of her eager yearning for God, filled me with love. We were here, together, sharing in a baptism that was so intimate and yet so open before God.

"Have you accepted the Lord Jesus as your personal savior?" I asked her, in the traditional words of baptism.

"Yes," she said softly.

"And you'd like to follow the Lord's command and be baptized?"

"Yes," she answered.

"I baptize you, Rita, in the name of the Father, and of the Son, and of the Holy Spirit." Gently, I held her in one arm and lowered her into the water, and watched as the water closed in over her face. Then I lifted her up again, and as she emerged from the water, a glow spread over her face. I saw tears mingling with the water, but they were tears of joy.

I pulled her into my arms, and we knelt there in the water silently, holding each other close.

7

"The World Turns Against Us"

As the weeks went on, the more we were together, the more we grew as one. Although we weren't married yet, we felt like we were married in spirit.

And everything seemed so perfect. Each day brought new decisions about setting up the home that would be ours and about how to serve the church best. I tried to think of all the ways we could make the parsonage our home. There were colors to choose and curtains to match. The porch could be converted into an office for Norman and I could already visualize the best places for plants and paintings. I couldn't wait for the cherry blossoms to bloom on the enormous tree in the back yard.

I really wanted the parsonage to be a warm and comfortable place where the congregation would feel free to visit. As I dusted off my collection of cookbooks, I grew happy thinking that I would soon get the chance to make my favorite recipes.

I wanted to know everything about being a good pastor's

wife. What a responsibility! There would be people to meet and activities to join. It was awesome, and it was exciting. I've always been a "people person," and the role of pastor's wife was one I would relish. Uppermost in my mind were the young people, and I was happy that we already got along well. They were fascinated by the soap opera, but I was able to share with them the thought that real happiness comes from knowing Jesus.

Sunday mornings were filled with encouragement and support from the congregation. I was happy, especially for Norman, that the people were responding to me so well. Each week when I walked into church for the morning service, I'd recognize more faces and remember the names that went with them. The people were warm and loving, and several would say, "Rita, sit here with us."

After the choir sang and it was time for Norman to begin his sermon, a thrill would run through me. Everyone knew that this man of God was an anointed preacher. And I was to be his wife!

To me, things couldn't have been better. But I began to sense in Norman that there was something wrong. As the pastor, Norman was getting signs that I was unaware of. There were those among the church leadership who were concerned that because I had been raised a Catholic I wouldn't make a good wife for a Baptist minister. They also questioned whether an actress could fulfill all her church responsibilities. Wouldn't an actress taint the ministry? Unfortunately, rumors began to spread and words were twisted.

Even though to this day I believe in my heart that God could have made me an effective pastor's wife, the considerations of the church are understandable. It would have taken the incomprehensible wisdom of God for everyone to understand the situation. And if the Lord had wanted to make people understand, they would have.

A few days after we announced our engagement to the applause of the congregation, we met with the church board. They asked if we intended to become members of the church.

Norman answered that a pastor and his wife could best serve a church by being members. We told them that we were in full agreement with the doctrinal statement of the church and were completely comfortable in preaching it. At the same time, we made it clear that it was not our ministry to put down any other religion or denomination. After all, it had been in the Catholic Church that I had come to a saving knowledge of Jesus.

After considering the matter, a board member told us that if they had known I was to be Norman's wife they would never have voted him in as pastor in the first place. At that point, another board member recommended that we quietly look for another church. Not all of the members felt that way, but only one young deacon openly stood with us and supported our ministry.

However, because the majority felt the way they did, we knew we could never serve there effectively. The next Sunday, Norman announced his resignation to the congregation. They were shocked. No one could understand what had happened. They felt both sadness and a sense of rejection. Although a few of them knew that there had been problems, they felt that we were running out on them.

After the service, a woman came up to me with tears in her eyes and said, "Don't you realize, you're ruining a great ministry?"

The whole story will never be told, and we know that's the way the Lord wants it. It is in the best interest of the church family as a whole for us not to go into everything that happened behind the scenes.

With good intentions, the congregation immediately organized a meeting to override Norman's decision to resign. But we knew it was final. With a heavy heart, Norman stood up and said, "I'll always appreciate your vote of confidence, but if you really want to support me, then endorse my decision to leave."

Solemnly, the vote was taken and Norman's resignation was accepted.

Norman had gone alone to that final meeting before the church membership. Because I wasn't a member, I waited for him in the parsonage. I lowered the lights and lit some candles. In the background I put on an Evie Tornquist record and prayed. The music filled the room and helped focus my thoughts on God.

She sang about turning all your problems over to the Lord, and, hearing the comforting words, I closed my eyes and pictured the whole problem in my mind. I lifted my hands up as if giving the whole situation to Jesus.

God cared and I knew He would take care of everything. Although I didn't know how Norman was doing at the meeting, I knew that he would be okay. I knew that God would protect us both.

During the next few weeks before our final departure, it took every ounce of courage we had to face the congregation every Sunday. Standing in the pulpit, Norman would look out at all the faces of the people and see doubt. We realized that it was hopeless, that we might be able to clear up one rumor with one person, but we couldn't clear up all the rumors with everyone. The seed of doubt had been planted.

At our lowest points, Norman and I came to learn how much the Psalms were written for us. The more we prayed and looked to the Bible for strength, the more we were given solace and confirmation that what we were doing was right before God.

In Psalm 37 we found God's answer: "Commit everything you do to the Lord. Trust Him to help you do it and He will. Your innocence will be clear to everyone. He will vindicate you with the blazing light of justice shining down as from the noonday sun" (*The Living Bible*).

We didn't need to worry about proving ourselves right. God would take care of it for us. Knowing that, we tried during the days and weeks that followed to reach out to everyone in the church, whether they were with us or not. "Oh Lord, please teach us to forgive," we'd pray. We knew that the love of Christ could touch them, and we needed to be the instrument of that love.

The pressures and frustrations of these weeks drew Norman and me together even more. While everything around us was trying to tear us apart, we were held close by our love for each other and our love for God.

During those weeks of turmoil, it was so comforting to know that I had a strong, confident man I could lean on. And I respected Norman's judgment so much. No matter what difficulties arose, he emphasized how much we had going for us, and how we could work out every problem with God's love.

And, along with the church problem, there were others, especially from my family. Before we announced our engagement, I was under tremendous pressure at home to put off our engagement and the wedding.

"Why rush it?" my mother would say.

The pressures intensified during a three-week trip to Hawaii that my mother and I took in late September. Early in the year the show had allotted this time for my vacation and the plans were all set months before I met Norman. He had suggested that we get engaged before the trip, but my mother urged, "Why not wait until you come back. You'll only be gone three weeks."

I wanted to please everybody, and I ended up pleasing no one. I wanted so much to marry Norman right away, but I didn't want to hurt my mother, who had always been close to me. She had also been my manager, and my adviser; we always traveled together and shared everything.

So Norman and I decided it would be better to wait and announce the engagement when we got back. First my mother and I went to California, where I appeared on two religious TV specials for George Otis, and then we flew to Hawaii for the vacation. Those were the longest three weeks of my life. I had hoped that this would be a time of renewed closeness between my mother and me. We'd have time to be alone and understand each other. But the more I tried to pull us together, the more we drifted apart. Something had happened. Our relationship wasn't the same anymore.

When we returned from Hawaii, there was Norman waiting for us at Kennedy Airport. I rushed into his arms and held him tight. Now that we were together again there was no reason at all to postpone our engagement.

Pressures from the church continued to mount. One night Norman was helping me rehearse a script in my home in Brooklyn. He often helped me with my scripts, but this was different. The scene was an argument between Carol and her second husband, Jay Stallings. Carol had just discovered that Jay was unfaithful again, and this time she had reached the breaking point.

"Get out of my life, get out of my life," I screamed at Norman, who was reading the part of Jay. "I never want to see you again."

"Don't say that—please don't say that," said Norman.

But those weren't Jay's lines. They were Norman's. He put the script down and said, "Listen, I can't handle this."

I hated to see Norman this way. I realized how much the pressures of the situation were getting to him. And I wondered whether I was doing the right thing for his sake to go along with this marriage.

In fact, one night in the parsonage, the music was playing softly and Norman and I were dancing slowly to the song "Feelings." As we held each other closely, he began softly singing along. When he came to the line about wishing he'd never met the girl, the words hit me, and I wondered if that's how he really felt. "He must—why would he say those words if he didn't mean them?" I held him even more tightly and my eyes filled with tears.

"What's the matter?" Norman asked.

"What you just said—that it would be better if you hadn't met me. It's true, isn't it?"

"Honey, those are the words to the song. You know I could never feel that way. I love you. The Lord has great plans for us. Believe me, things will work out."

He was so strong, so assured, that it made me feel confident too.

We decided to postpone the wedding until May, and I thought that my home problems would clear up, but things became more and more tense. Where once my mother and I had been very close, now we were acting like strangers.

"Everyone at work is thrilled I've met the man I'm going to marry," I said. "They know how long I've wanted to get married and that I was waiting for the right person. Now that he's here, I want you to be as happy as I am."

More and more of the time that Norman and I were together was spent talking about my family. What got me through those times when I was sure that my family didn't love me or care was the strength of his love. No matter how beaten down he was by his church, he put me and my family problems first. I would be in tears. "I can't understand how they can feel this way." And with whatever energy he had, he comforted me. He was always there when I needed him.

But as much as he consoled me, never once did he say, "You're right—your family doesn't love you," even though that would have been the easy way out. Instead, he'd calm me down and say, "Rita, they love you very much. They're going through a hard time themselves when they think about losing you. But they love you."

Just as he was helping me love my family at a time when it was difficult, he was also helping me to grow up and face responsibilities for making my own decisions. I had been so close to my family as I was growing up that we had never disagreed on anything important. As a result, I had never really become an adult, where I made my own decisions and stuck by them. Even when it came to deciding about my own marriage, I was torn by indecision. When it came to setting an earlier date, I bounced back and forth between following what my mother wanted and doing what Norman and I wanted.

"There comes a time in your life when you have to decide for yourself," Norman told me. "When you look back on your life, you can't blame your mother or anyone else for the way your life turned out. You have to choose your own course, and take the risk, and accept responsibility for whatever you do."

I took the first steps toward maturity one afternoon, when I was torn up by my mother's problems and was feeling very deeply for the struggle she was going through over my marriage. At the same time, I was torn by such indecision that I actually thought there was no way for me to ever break free of the emotional strain I was feeling from my family.

Part of me loved my mother so much and wanted her approval for what I was doing. Another part of me hated the fact that I was more controlled by her than she would ever really want me to be, if she weren't caught up in her feelings. I would be influenced by what she'd tell me, and then wonder what was the right thing to do.

"Oh, Norman," I said. "I'm never going to be free to respond on my own," but at that moment I realized just what I was saying. If it were true, Norman and I would never have a chance for real happiness. And that realization shook me out of my indecision. His words came back to me: "You have to choose your own course, and take the risk, and accept responsibility for whatever you do."

That was the turning point. I was in danger of losing the treasure of my life. Many times before, my work, my school, and my family pressures had intervened in relationships and they didn't work out. But with Norman, I knew I had found the "pearl of great price" and there was no way I was going to risk losing him.

I wanted my mother with me. But more than anything I wanted to marry Norman. There was one thing I was sure of, and that was that he loved me totally and would stand by me forever.

I told myself, "I've got to fight this. I've got to break out of the role I've gotten into with my family. I can't please everybody. Now is the time to do what I think is right."

I told Norman, "I can't live without you. I don't know how

it's going to work, but if you're willing to hang in there with me, I'm going to make this work. I'm going to ask God to confirm my decision and let me know without a shadow of a doubt that it's His will."

By now, we were talking about an earlier wedding, in February instead of May, so I turned it over to the Lord. I wrote in my diary:

"Dear Jesus, I love You so much. Please help me to know Your will. I want only Your will. It seems so right to move up the wedding date. We have no reason to wait until May. Especially since we wouldn't get any more support if we did.

"God, show me the way. I want to do the right thing. I want to support Norman and be with him, especially living through these difficult times. And it hurts so much to leave each other at night. It's not sex, Lord, that's not the reason we want to get married. It's that we simply want to be together. We feel You've given us a special love, and a special ministry.

"As I write to You, Lord, I feel so strongly that February is a good time to get married. But I want to wait upon You, and pray and listen to You speak. I thank You so much, Lord, for Your love and for this peace which I feel bursting in my heart right now.

"Thank You, Jesus, for dying for me and for sending me Norman. How I love him. Make me worthy of his love, and mold me into the kind of Christian wife You want me to be—loving, supportive, kind and charming and selfless. I want to be better. Please help me. I'm up to 131 pounds again—help me lose it, Lord.

"I trust You, Father God. Thank You for the peace. Love your child, Rita. Thank You, Lord. I feel so good."

And then I went on:

"God, I want a sign. I want it to be very clear. I want You to tell me exactly what I should do. I'll do Your will, even if it means waiting a couple of months. But let me know."

A few days later I got my sign in a way that was totally unexpected. One evening I was at home and my mother said, "Rita, I'm going to risk losing you by telling you this, but we've got to have a talk." I sat down and didn't say a word as she read off a list of reasons why we should put off the marriage until May. For forty minutes she recounted the reasons. "How will you ever find any congregation that wants a pastor's wife who's on TV? You'd never be able to travel the way you do now."

I had heard all of these objections so many times before, but for the first time I heard clearly what she was saying. She wasn't telling me to wait. Whether she realized it or not, she was telling me to put off the wedding—permanently. Her intensity revealed more than just a mother's natural concerns for her daughter who was getting married. I knew she wasn't acting like herself at all, and at twenty-five I had to do what I felt was right.

At that moment I was more sure than ever. "Thank You, God, for this sign. I didn't know it was going to be so clear. It hurt. But thank You." I went into my room and called Norman. "We have to talk."

It was early December, and Norman and I met at a cozy corner table in the Coffee Cafe in Rockefeller Center. From our table we could see the ice skaters twirling around the rink. The giant tree was already lighted up for Christmas, and the whole scene was beautiful.

"Norman, if we eloped," I said intently, "when would be the soonest we could do it?"

"This Saturday," Norman said without hesitation.

"You're not helping me," I said. "I'm under a lot of pressure and I want to know what you think. Please be serious."

"I *am* being serious," he said, feeling the pressure that he was under himself. "I've known our marriage is right for five months now. All I'm saying is that I'm more than ready anytime you are. If you find that disturbing, I'm sorry."

We spent the next few moments in tense silence as the ice skaters happily circled the rink to familiar Christmas carols. Somehow the music and the laughter made the moment even sadder. After Norman paid the check, we quietly walked out into the busy shopping arcade in the RCA Building. At one point we stopped and turned toward each other. We both wanted to make another attempt to understand.

"Pardon me, can I have your autograph?" I turned to see a pleasant little woman standing behind me. "I just saw a show on Broadway, and it would really make my trip to New York if you would sign the *Playbill*."

We both smiled and I introduced her to Norman. "I'd be happy to," I said.

"I hope I haven't disturbed you," she said apologetically, "but I just had to talk to you."

"Not at all," Norman said. She waved and in seconds she disappeared into the crowd.

"I'm sorry I jumped on you, honey," he said. "I know you need me to be understanding. I'm really sorry, sweetheart."

"Oh, Norman," I said, looking into his eyes, "I'm the one who's sorry. You are always understanding."

All the reasons we should wait to get married didn't hold up against the reasons to go ahead immediately. By the end of the day we had decided to elope in two weeks.

The next few days were filled with accomplishing all the things that the law requires—blood tests, a marriage license.

We took out our license at a little marriage license bureau, and even the application process was fun. My friend Marsha came with us as a witness. She has such a good sense of humor that before we got to the bureau we were laughing at everything. Norman turned to us and said, "All I ask is that when you get inside, please don't kid around. This is a city office and, believe me, they take their business seriously."

At the bureau the clerk who was to handle our application introduced herself as "Mrs. Chestnut." Norman looked at Marsha and me, but we remained straight-faced. As she proceeded through the questions on the form, each one seemed to strike us all funny. But we kept our responses to a dignified smile. Finally, Mrs. Chestnut looked at Marsha and said, "As their witness, you must answer the following question. To your knowledge, is either of these individuals an imbecile?"

At that, we all broke up—with Norman laughing the

loudest. When we left, Mrs. Chestnut wished us well and
Marsha and I told Norman that in the future he should act
more seriously in a city office building.

On Saturday, December 11, 1976, we were married in a little church in North Bergen, New Jersey. The minister, Pastor
Wilcomes, was a friend Norman had met four years before at
a seminar.

Our wedding was small and lovelier than we could have
imagined. I wore a simple short white dress. There was no
crowd of guests—only my friend Marsha, her boy friend
Damon, and Pastor Wilcomes and his wife Emma. On the
way to the church we bought two long-stemmed blue roses
for Marsha and Emma and one long-stemmed white rose for
me. As it turned out, both Marsha and Emma happened to
wear long blue gowns.

And there was love. It filled every corner of the church.
You could feel it outside the church in the dazzling beauty of
that frosty afternoon. The trees around the church glistened
with icicles, creating a magical wonderland. You could feel it
inside the church, in the cozy warmth created by the Christmas decorations and from the marvelous aroma of the turkey
that was roasting in Mrs. Wilcomes' oven. The dining room of
the parsonage was through a door near the altar, and the cook-
ing scents came from the reception dinner that Mrs. Wilcomes
was preparing for us.

Sunlight was streaming through the windows as Norman
flipped on the tape recorder to begin the wedding march. He
stood in front, next to Pastor Wilcomes. I marched down the
aisle, carrying one long-stemmed white rose, following Marsha
and Emma. Although the church was empty, in my heart it
seemed filled to overflowing.

My heart was pounding. But Norman didn't look nervous at
all. He was totally composed. And when he spoke, it was as if
he were a movie actor, playing the most romantic role in the
world.

Pastor Wilcomes opened the service, looking out over the

congregation of empty pews, wanting to give the impression that the church was filled.

Norman repeated after him in a slow, loving voice. "I, Norman, in the presence of God and these witnesses . . ." he started to say. I felt like melting on the spot. He was so beautiful. He gazed into my eyes as he said the words—and I saw his large blue eyes, so tender and strong. He was everything I wanted my groom to be.

" . . . take thee Rita, to be my wedded wife." I could feel the tears roll down my cheeks as he said those words I had thought I might never hear from him.

"And I plight thee my troth through all eternity."

"Through all eternity," I thought. When it was my turn to repeat the vows, my voice was hoarse, and I was choked up with emotion.

Pastor Wilcomes infused every moment with deep meaning and love. When he asked for the rings, he said, "These rings represent your endless love and fidelity, a symbol of the love that is complete, beautiful and endless. May God help you to make your love perfect and eternal."

Together we knelt on the homemade white satin pillow that Pastor and Mrs. Wilcomes had used in their wedding. We prayed together, and then came the words that made my heart leap.

"I now pronounce you man and wife."

Norman took me in his arms and kissed me tenderly, as the tape-recorded music swelled with the sounds of "O Holy Night."

With one simple ceremony I was married. It happened just like that. I kept looking at my wedding ring and saying over and over to myself, "I'm Mrs. Walter."

Our reception was as loving and homey as our wedding. Mrs. Wilcomes had the dining room table overflowing with food: turkey, stuffing, potatoes—the works. We all sat around the table like a family, joking and having a good time. A few hours later, Marsha, Damon, Norman, and I left for Manhattan. After dropping them off, Norman and I went on to the Essex House on Central Park South for our one-night honeymoon.

Everything we loved about New York seemed to be summed up by having a room with a park view, and Norman had paid eighty-two dollars in advance the week before to be sure that we got one. But when we opened the door to the room, the only view was a brick wall. I was all in favor of keeping it—I didn't want to make any trouble. But Norman insisted that we do things right. And despite the fact that the lobby was filled with conventioneers, Norman stood up to the manager and we got our room with the view of Central Park.

"Wow," I thought, "as a husband, he's really going to be something."

As happy as we were, we knew that there was one thing I had to do before I could feel at peace. I had to call my mother to tell her that we had eloped.

I picked up the phone and dialed. When my mom answered, I said, "Uh, Mom . . . there's . . . uh . . . something I have to tell you." With that the phone went dead.

I dialed again. "Mom, what I wanted to say was . . ."

She could sense the seriousness in my voice. "Why are you telling me this now?" she broke in. "Tell me when . . ." but again we were disconnected. What a time for the phone company to give me trouble.

As I redialed, I looked at Norman in exasperation. "I can't believe this! If I ever saw this on TV I'd say it would never happen in real life!" I finally got her on the line again and blurted it out.

"You know how much I told you I wanted to get married, and you said, 'Why not elope if you're in such a hurry?' Well . . . we did. We got married today."

At first there was silence. And then my mother said, "Just this morning I told Auntie you were going to do that. God be with you."

We waited till the new week to tell Norman's parents. His

mother had gone on a trip to Acapulco, and we wanted to wait till his mom and dad were together. They had always been supportive and we joked with his mom, "You didn't know it, but you were in Acapulco taking our honeymoon for us."

Ours may be the only wedding night in the world where the groom had to stay up and go over his sermon notes for the next day. He got up at 5 a.m. to go over the notes again. I got up with him and called room service for breakfast. Then we got ready for church and went to New Jersey.

I could feel my heart beating as I walked into church, keeping our secret hidden. No one noticed the rings on our fingers. Norman opened the service with a hymn. At the end he paused.

"Before we go any further, I have an announcement to make. Yesterday, Rita and I were married." After a moment he said, "Shall we bow our heads for our morning prayer."

Norman bowed his head and began to pray. When he finished, he waited for the usual choral response from the choir. But they didn't make a sound. I raised my head and looked around me. Everyone seemed frozen with their eyes fixed on Norman. The organ didn't play, the choir didn't sing.

As the news began to sink in, faces turned toward me with smiles and nods of congratulations. And although our future was unsure, we knew that God was in control and we would always be together.

8

"I'm Not a Minister Anymore"

The church board and I had mutually agreed that Rita and I would leave the parsonage by February 7. I had wanted to see the congregation through the holidays because Christmas is such an important time in the life of a church. But in my heart I left that church earlier on a bleak, cold Sunday in January. It was early morning, before the Sunday service, and I was sitting alone in the living room by the fireplace. Rita was upstairs getting dressed for church. I looked around the familiar room, and I realized that all that was left of our ministry was to move out of the parsonage with our belongings.

For the first time it hit me. "I'm not a minister anymore."

Stories would spread quickly. No church would hire me. My reputation was ruined. In a short time each of these fears would be confirmed.

I could feel the tears welling up in my eyes, and my chest felt like it was caving in. I couldn't stop it. These were the tears of weeks in turmoil. I hadn't wept like that since I was a kid.

As the tears came pouring out, the memories of my ministry came rushing back. I remembered my longings as a boy to be a minister and to preach from the pulpit. I remembered my first five years as a minister in Jersey City, where I had been captain of the ship, making decisions, leading a congregation, and filling them with God's love. I had had a love affair with that church and with that city. I saw the faces of the people in that little church. To them I was still "Pastor." How I missed them all at that moment. I wondered what they had heard about me, but I knew they would stand with me.

And then God had given me the chance to move to this church in the suburbs. I had come to love many here and I had also felt the rejection of some. But through it all I had felt the joy and fulfillment of being a minister, of doing God's work from the pulpit.

Every week as a minister I had been caught up in that "Sunday morning feeling" I had when I stepped into the pulpit and faced the congregation. Seeing the faces of people, needing to be filled with the Word of God, gave me energy and strength. It was a feeling I could never forget.

Those same people who filled the church on Sunday mornings called me when they needed help or when their lives were in bits and pieces. They called to ask their pastor to hold the pieces together for them, and to listen.

The ministry was my life, not my job.

As I sat on the sofa thinking about all these things, a sense of deep tragedy came over me. My grief wasn't just because I wouldn't be preaching on Sunday, or because I wasn't going to be getting a paycheck anymore. I wept because all that I was and wanted to be for the Lord and for Rita was falling apart.

People wouldn't be calling me anymore. The phone wouldn't ring anymore with someone saying, "Come over right away, my husband's arguing with the lady downstairs." I used to laugh when some people called me if they had a problem with their gas bill. But I loved it.

And now it was gone.

"Lord, You know I love Rita so much. She is so precious to me."

I stopped for a moment because it's hard to pray when you're really broken. "I know You're going to help us, Lord, but, oh God, this hurts."

"I love you," God answered. "The world rejected Me also. My grace is sufficient for you. I will see you through."

"But Lord, where am I headed? I never dreamed I'd face something like this. How can I ever start all over again even if I get the chance?"

His words remained: "I love you . . . My grace is sufficient for you." So without promise of future success, He lifted me up from the depths. On that memorable Sunday morning He reminded me not to look to anyone but Him for acceptance or approval.

"Thank You, Jesus," I said. "Please help me to trust You through this thing."

In a few minutes my eyes were dry and my normal color returned. Down the carpeted steps came the beautiful angel of God in my life, dressed and ready for church. Rita smiled and said, "Can I help you with anything, sweetheart?"

I returned her smile. Just having her there was what I needed.

During the first few weeks after we left the church, I was too busy to feel the full impact of my changed role. We moved to Manhattan, and much of my time was spent getting organized and acclimated to the exciting pace of the city. I loved New York more than any other place in the world, and I was thrilled to be there with the woman I loved.

But on Sundays I'd feel the emptiness again, especially when we visited other churches to find a place where we felt comfortable worshiping. One service in particular brought all my feelings of loss to the surface.

It started out positively enough: the music was lovely and the Gospel reading that day was powerful. But when it came time for the sermon, the minister delivered a dull, dry message. The more I listened to him, the more frustrated I got. I looked around and saw a congregation of people who needed to hear the Word of God. Instead, they heard a lifeless sermon with no mention of Jesus—no mention of the saving power of Christ that could give new direction to their lives.

As the organ swelled with a closing hymn, I wanted to shout: "Wait, wait!" But I walked out, empty inside.

What also hurt was my loss of prestige. The position of minister is respected in almost any group. When I had a church, I could walk into a group and instantly be surrounded by dozens of people who wanted to talk to me. Now, in those same groups, no one seemed to care about me. It was as if overnight I had become a nobody.

As time went on, my day-to-day world began to deteriorate. I remember once asking a member of my congregation how he liked his new life of retirement. He looked at me and said, "Pastor, I have the horrible feeling that I'm just wasting time."

That's how I began to feel. In the church I had left, I had been senior pastor, with two ministers under me and with responsibility for a large physical plant and the spiritual needs of several hundred people. A minister's job is an executive position, and I had treated it that way.

On Monday mornings I'd be in the office early to think about new ideas for the church, take calls and organize the administrative tasks in the life of the growing congregation.

In the church, I had been in an office, making critical decisions, and I had substantial things to be concerned about. Now, for all practical purposes, I was unemployed at the age of twenty-nine. And now that I didn't have the real responsibilities of an executive, I was on edge all the time. I started worrying about meaningless things, things that would never have bothered me before. If Rita and I were late for an appointment or had to cancel a speaking engagement, I'd become overwrought.

One of my biggest fears was for Rita's safety. Whenever she left the apartment to go to the store, I'd caution her, "Don't forget to wear your scarf and dark glasses." When she did forget, I'd say, "Do you have to go like that? You look just like Carol Stallings."

My worst fears were confirmed one night after I came in from taking out the garbage. I had left the apartment door unlocked as I went to get another bag from the kitchen. When I turned around, I saw a man walking in the door.

I slammed the door in his face and heard his feet running down the hall.

"How can I ever let Rita be alone?" I thought. "Whenever I have to walk down to the laundry room or go out shopping, I won't be able to relax again."

I was convinced that my nights of sleep were over. I might have realized that perhaps the man had made a mistake and he had started running because I had scared him. But to me it signaled the worst as far as Rita's safety was concerned. Just when my fear of the crime in the city and of our vulnerability was the greatest, another unsettling incident occurred.

Someone had used my credit card number to run up a six-hundred-dollar bill on our account. Surely, the next step would be that we would be robbed of even more—perhaps of even our lives. And the theft started to eat away at me. "Someone knows our credit card number," I thought. "And six hundred dollars is gone—just like that."

I was angry and frustrated by my inability to control the situation. And I was so busy focusing on the credit card that I lost sight of something even more important—God.

"It's not important, Norman," Rita said. "Don't worry about it." Ironically, those were the very words I had heard her speak to her TV husband, Jay, that morning when he discovered that an employee was bilking him of thousands of dollars. Jay had said, "Don't you realize he's robbing me blind?" And Carol had calmed him down and helped him put the theft in perspective, just as Rita was doing for me.

Rita followed with words that were even more familiar. She repeated one of my sermons back to me.

"You know how you always say that you're really doing the Lord's work when Satan starts attacking," she reminded me. "Well, you must be doing something right because he's really got you now.

"He knows where we're weakest. And right now, privacy and my safety are where you're most vulnerable. Stop for a minute and think about who really controls our lives and even our credit card. It's God. Let's put it in His hands."

Hearing her words reminded me that I was in the midst of a struggle, not with the person who stole six hundred dollars with our credit card number, but with Satan. He was the unseen enemy, and I had allowed myself to get off the track, to focus on the human enemy, rather than on God's power to control the forces of evil.

"This could only have happened because God has allowed it to happen," said Rita. "There must be a reason!"

We prayed for God to help us understand what the loss of the money meant, and even more what the loss of my ministry meant.

During those long weeks and months without a full-time ministry, I clung to one of the status symbols of a busy, working person—a suit and tie. When I was a minister, I had always worn a jacket and tie because so much of my work required it. Even though I was no longer a minister, I would get up in the morning and put on a shirt and tie. I guess it was my way of holding on to a world that I was no longer part of.

Whenever I went out, even if it was just to go to the post office or the supermarket, I put on a suit and carried an attaché case. Rita knew how important it was for me to look respectable. As I was going out the door to shop, she'd smile and say, "You know, before I was married, I always pictured that my husband would have a suit and tie and briefcase."

She was the one I cared about. I didn't care about impressing the lady in the grocery store or the clerk in the post office. I cared about Rita. And she was confirming to me that she didn't think I was crazy. Although there was nothing in that attaché case except the shopping list and the morning newspaper, I felt that I was giving Rita a part of a man she could be proud of.

I often wondered why God had brought me to this low point, why He had permitted my ministry to be taken away and had left me without anything to fall back on. I believed that God had called me to preach. And just as deeply I believed that He had brought Rita and me together. But for what purpose? Where was it all leading?

Back when I had my church, I had faced a fork in the road. Down one road were the church leaders, telling me that my role as a minister should be to follow their directives and that my marriage to Rita was wrong. And when I had looked down the other road, I saw Rita, who I knew had been brought to me by God. And down that same road I saw Christ leading both of us.

I chose the road that was not the "approved" way—the way approved by men. And I realized then that I couldn't live my life according to what looked good, or seemed good, or even what my background said was good. I had to live my life based on what God told me was right.

I decided it was time to start piecing my career together again. Sure, I wouldn't start at the top, but lots of churches in the area needed assistant pastors. Several pastors knew me personally and they knew my work. Unfortunately, each one had heard stories about us and no minister wanted to invite division in his church.

One day I received a call from a pastor who had heard about us from other ministers. I had come to expect another discouraging lecture at this point. Instead, he said, "Would you and Rita come and speak at my church? I understand you sing, too." Praise the Lord! I thought we could fit that in.

It was a small friendly church and everyone welcomed us

warmly. During the service Rita and I sang a hymn and then she gave her testimony. Next it was my turn to give a message.

It felt so good to be looking at those faces again, to be talking about Jesus and offering Him to all who wanted to receive Him. At the close of my sermon I gave an invitation. "If God has spoken to your heart this morning, and you would like to accept the Lord Jesus into your life, I'm going to ask you to raise your hand so I can pray with you."

Then a strange and wonderful thing happened. More people from that little group responded than had answered any other invitation I had ever given before. And as I stepped down into the congregation, many came forward to receive Christ.

I looked over at the pastor, with his church, with his "Sunday morning feeling" that I loved, and I couldn't help thinking, "I wonder if you know how lucky you are. I hope you realize all that God has given you, and how much you would miss it if it were taken away."

Finally I got to the point where I decided to volunteer as a minister in other churches. After all, God had blessed us with a salary to live on through Rita's career. Why not offer a ministry to others for nothing?

That's what I had in mind the day I had lunch with the area director of a large group of Baptist churches. It was late spring in New York. As I walked along Broadway toward Seventy-ninth Street, the sun was shining and the air was surprisingly fresh. Today would be a new beginning.

The conversation seemed to be going along fine. My host was relaxed and congenial as I explained my problems with my church, and made it clear that I didn't hold it against them. I told him of my desire to preach, and my eagerness to get involved in a full-time ministry again. I made it clear that I was offering my services free of charge because I wanted so much to be doing God's work.

He nodded and smiled, and I felt confident that, finally, things were going to work out. But when the luncheon drew to a close, no offer had come up. And I began to suspect that something had gone wrong.

"Thanks for coming, Norman," he said, giving me a friendly pat on the back. "We'll give you a call if something comes up."

I could feel my heart fall at his words. Once I had been in demand as a preacher, and I had been building a career for God. Now, to have offered myself for free, and to have been turned down, was more than I could handle.

"I'm worth less than nothing," I thought, as the bus approached my stop. I got off at Forty-ninth Street and walked around Times Square for hours desperately trying to feel like a part of the stream of things.

But Rita wouldn't let me wallow in my rejection. She always believed in me. When she got home from the studio, I told her about being turned down by the churches. She reminded me of the positive things I had going for me. "You still have your radio ministry, and you still have all those people in the nursing home who count on you every week," she said. "What you do for those people is ten times more valuable than what I do. I know your preaching blesses their hearts. Look how their numbers have grown since you started preaching there. Look how their faces light up when you walk in their rooms.

"I know God has something waiting for you," she would say. "Something great is just around the corner."

When I'd hear her talk, I couldn't stay down for long. And I started to look forward to my Tuesday meetings with the senior citizens even more. Since I didn't have a weekly Sunday sermon to rely on for notes at the nursing home, I began to speak without notes at all. I found I could stand up and preach a whole message. All I needed was a passage from the Bible.

One day as I was on my way home from an afternoon of preaching, I understood what that meant. "Do you realize—you've never been able to do that—to preach extemporaneously before a group!" I said to myself.

In the years when I had a church, I had prepared my sermons diligently by sitting down with my Bible, thinking of illustrations, using cross-references from commentaries and things I had read. It was like putting together a meal in the kitchen, taking an ingredient from here and another from there.

Now I had no ready-made ingredients. God was requiring me to live off the land. I had to use my faith in that nursing home and every ounce of the background He had given me. Sometimes in my church, life had almost been too easy, and I was getting fat like a sponge, soaking everything in. Now God was saying, "I'm going to put you on red alert. You're going to start using everything I've given you."

At the same time that God was stretching my preaching skills, He was testing me in other ways. Because I was leading a life of retirement, by necessity I was thrown into closer contact with Rita's career. I became her manager, a job her mother had handled for years. That meant arranging for publicity interviews, making contacts with talent agents who wanted her for commercials, setting up personal appearances. I was learning about show business firsthand.

I even got my first taste of acting. "As the World Turns" was looking for someone to play the part of a minister, and the producer suggested me. I played myself, Rev. Norman Walter, and my job was to marry Carol Ann (Annie) and Beau.

My nervousness started a week before taping, when I got the script. There were four pages to memorize. I had never been good at memorization. In fact, I used to freeze in every school play and I couldn't memorize a sermon—I always used notes. They were one-word notes like an outline, but they always kept me on the right track.

But now I had to appear before eight million people and remember four solid pages of script. It was like a monologue because I had all the lines except for a couple of "I do's." What's more, I was coming on the show as Rita's husband, and everybody in the cast knew me. She had spoken of me so highly at the studio that I didn't want to do anything to disappoint her.

The morning of my TV debut Rita and I reversed roles. Every other morning it was Rita who got out of bed and went to the studio. That morning I was the one who went. And Rita stayed home, mercifully, so that I could make my own mistakes.

The first thing we did in the studio was run through the lines. Everyone on the show was wonderful and they had all known me for a long time. The director, Len, was a good friend who had encouraged our romance. But when it's time to work, the warm, friendly atmosphere fades and the studio is like a pressure cooker. In the midst of this tension, I decided I wouldn't do a thing unless I was spoken to.

Len said to the cast, "Okay, everyone, let's do it." And I stood there, waiting.

He looked at me impatiently, and said, "Well, *read* the script." I had been waiting for a cue, for him to say, "Norman, you talk now." Instead, he had expected me to jump right in and say my lines.

The only thing that saved the day for me was that Len used me almost as technical adviser for the wedding scene. He continually asked me whether the service was right, and he'd change it according to my suggestions. For example, in the script, the minister asked, "Who gives this woman to be married to this man?" And the father answered, "I do."

Len asked me, "Is that the way you would do it?"

"I'd usually say, 'Her mother and I do,'" I said. So they changed the lines in the script. I felt great giving this kind of advice—it was something I was familiar with. All I wanted was to stay technical adviser and forget my acting job.

After a couple of rehearsals in the big empty room known as the rehearsal hall, we went up on the set to run through it again before final taping. When I walked on the set, I immediately felt right at home. A little church was set up in the studio, and it looked remarkably like my first church in Jersey City. But I would have felt even more comfortable if I had been performing a real wedding ceremony. I was beginning to perspire as I thought about having to get every line right, and

I panicked thinking that every quiver of my nostril would be recorded on camera. There would be no distance between me and the "congregation" as there was in a real church. The camera would bring me face to face with all those people watching from their living rooms.

What made my agony even worse was that I was acting in front of the principal characters on "As the World Turns." As we took our places on the set, I realized that I was looking into the faces of all those famous actors and actresses I had seen as a kid when my mother watched the show. I looked at Nancy Hughes and remembered seeing her humming "Oklahoma" on the show years before. Then there was Kathy Hays, who not only was one of my mother's favorites but was also a favorite of mine when she appeared on "Star Trek." And in front of me, too, were Don MacLaughlin, Patsy Bruder, Henderson Forsythe—it was overwhelming.

Before we ran through the scene, Len announced to the visitors, "Sorry, we have to ask all visitors on the set to leave." I had been a visitor so many times myself that for a second I thought I should be getting up and leaving too. A little while later, I wished I had. We went through the rehearsal on the set, and Len sat down with a list of "notes"—or criticisms—for each of the actors before the final taping. For some reason, he had notes for everyone else, but none for me.

"I must be so terrible they don't even want to tell me," I thought.

When we got in front of the camera for the taping, my adrenalin was flowing. I knew I had my lines down pat and I was charged up and ready to deliver them. The scene opened, and the wedding guests were escorted to their pews. I delivered my opening lines, and then moved into the wedding vows for Beau and his bride, Carol Ann.

I looked at the bride and said, "Do you, Mary Anne . . ."

A look of shock spread over the bride's face and I knew I was in trouble. Seconds later a voice sang over the intercom. "Norman," said Len, "all day, all night, it's *not* Mary Anne."

"Oh, please, Len, give me another chance," I said in a mock tone of pleading, hoping to relieve the tension.

"Let's take it from the top," he said. Now I was under double pressure. I had made a mistake on the very first page of the script. I had three more pages to go, and this time I had to get it perfect. I got through it without a slip-up, but I was convinced that I had done the worst job in the history of "As the World Turns."

Later that night Rita and I had dinner at a pleasant little restaurant on First Avenue. She asked me a hundred questions about my day, to which I gave empty, one-word answers. I was in temporary shock but I had a new, unforgettable appreciation for Rita's talent and career.

I had to admit, though, that being on the show had stimulated my interest in getting more involved in show business. To increase my chances, I took a soap opera acting course and some voice lessons. Several months later, they paid off when I had another shot at acting as an extra on another daytime series, "One Life to Live." I played a doctor, and although I didn't have any lines, I was called back two or three times to repeat the role and to play the part of a restaurant patron.

As an extra, you're low man on the totem pole, and I felt like it. At "As the World Turns" I had been a principal and I was Rita's husband. On this show I was on my own. Strangely enough, however, soon after my first appearance on the show, they hired an actor for a new principal role on the show. The actor was none other than Steve Bolster. Like a brother, he made me feel a part of the cast.

It was clearer than ever that God had not forgotten me. And I began to wonder what it all meant. It was fun and exciting to be on television. But I knew it didn't replace the thrill of stepping into a pulpit, seeing a congregation, and knowing that God had given me a message for them.

But God never let me lose sight of a preaching ministry. Even when I had no church, He filled my need. He used that time of uncertainty and doubt in my career to bring Rita and me closer together spiritually. We had no church, and we learned that our love would have to build its own cathedral.

God gave us that love, and He taught us to worship together in our married home. Rita had wanted me, her husband, to be the spiritual leader of our house. And so there, in our apartment, I found my pulpit. I became the pastor of a little church with a congregation of one.

On Sunday morning, we would sit on the edge of our bed, open our Bibles, and begin to read. On the side table we placed a communion cup and two little pieces of bread. Together, we would bow our heads and pray.

After I gave a little devotional, Rita would often contribute a thought that brought it all togeher. One of our concerns was about dieting.

"You know, Norman, when we get to heaven, God isn't going to ask us how much we weigh or how many pounds we lost. The Lord's only going to want to know whether we represented Him in this world and showed His love."

Our problem with dieting was just one of the battles we fought together during those little services in our bedroom cathedral. The biggest battle was learning to trust the Lord, day by day, minute by minute, through all the uncertainties about the future.

One morning as Rita and I talked about the battles we were confronting, I was struck by the thought that Christians are all part of God's powerful army. The general of an army doesn't want even one of his men killed or injured. God doesn't plan defeats, only victories, and His battle plans are perfect.

What God was telling me that morning was that the way to victory was to be obedient and trust Him. My life was by no means together, but God was showing me that He was in command, the battle was turning, and victory was sure.

I opened the Bible to Psalm 71, and there I found my past and my future summed up in the psalmist's words.

O God, from my youth thou has taught me,
and I still proclaim thy wondrous deeds.
So even to old age and gray hairs,
O God, do not forsake me,
till I proclaim thy might
to all the generations to come.

Thy power and thy righteousness, O God
  reach the high heavens.
Thou who hast done great things,
  O God, who is like thee?
Thou who hast made me see many sore troubles
  wilt revive me again;
   from the depths of the earth
   thou wilt bring me up again.
Thou wilt increase my honor, and comfort me again.

As I read the psalm aloud, I realized that, just as God had taught me in my youth, He was with me now, and would always be, even when my hair turned gray. But more than that, God was making clear to Rita and me that the future was ours.

"Did you hear what this is saying?" I asked Rita softly. "From the depths of the earth, thou will bring me up again. Thou will increase my honor, and comfort me again."

9

"Christ and Carol Stallings"

After I had signed literally hundreds of autographs at a personal appearance and Norm and I were on the way out, a woman stopped us and asked if I would sign "just one more autograph."

I smiled and said, "Sure." As I was signing it she commented, "I bet you get tired of people always coming up to meet you."

The fact is that it's the fans who have kept "As the World Turns" so popular for more than twenty-two years. Almost always the fans are polite and kind. Right now I correspond with more than seven hundred viewers, keeping them up to date on our activities and sending them recent pictures. I even keep a scrapbook of pictures they send me of themselves. Sometimes I get behind in my mail, and then I may spend a few weeks doing nothing but answering letters.

It's amazing how fans take a personal interest in my life. When I first got married, people in the business advised me not to use my married name because they were concerned that the fans would get confused. But I was so happy to be "Mrs. Walter" that I wanted everyone to know it. Well, the fans adjusted fast. Not only do I get letters addressed to "Rita Walter," but many are addressed, "Rev. and Mrs. Norman E. Walter."

I wonder sometimes if the fans realize how much their letters of support and encouragement mean. They may know Carol well and say things like "I'm just going to call you Carol." But after I meet them in person or exchange letters, they get to know Rita too. They know Carol has marriage troubles with Jay, but they know even more how happy Rita is with Norman.

In a sense, for the last nine years I've lived the ups and downs of Carol's life. When I get each script about a week in advance of taping, I immediately pore over it to see what's happened to Carol. Like the viewers, I don't know from week to week what the story of Carol's life will be. Reading a new script is almost like turning over a new page in my own life.

And what a life Carol has led! She's maturing, learning to take responsibility for herself, and becoming more aware of what the world is all about. She also has a deep need to give love and be liked. She's always been a "good" character— morally upright, vulnerable, and warm.

When I started on the show nine years ago, Carol was Carol Deming, a college student with a crush on a young law student named Tom Hughes. He wasn't very interested in dating, so Carol had to take the initiative. She left cookies at his house, gave him gifts on his birthday, and went out of her way to show she cared. Her father, Dr. Deming, a New York psychiatrist, never thought much of Tom. He saw a restlessness in him that he didn't like. But Carol persisted in loving him, even through a tragic trial where Tom was accused of murdering a man named Michael Shea. Tom had been seen leaving Shea's house the night of the murder. And Carol had overheard him say, "I'm going to get Michael Shea—I'm going to get him."

. . . with Archbishop Fulton J. Sheen and Carmel Quinn at a Catholic Actors Guild meeting.

Rita and TV husband Dennis Cooney on "The Mike Douglas Show." (Photo: Jason Bonderhoff, Courtesy *Daytime TV* and "The Mike Douglas Show").

Rita with "As the World Turns" director, Len Valenta, on the set.

Norman at work on his radio ministry. (Photo: Ronald Balsamo).

Rita with cast and crew of "As the World Turns" at a shower given for Rita.

Rita and Norman sharing their joint ministry. (Photo: Michael Moore)

A fan gathering. (Photo: John Hogan)

His light will shine forever. (Photo by Bill Stone)

The one person Carol loved she had to end up accusing on the witness stand in a tear-filled courtroom scene.

Later, Tom was pronounced innocent. At the same time, he also found a new romance—a girl named Meredith, who was frail and needed to be protected. A few weeks later Carol took off for New York to visit her father.

That's when I was written off the show. The new writers didn't know what to do with Carol's character. They weren't ready to have Tom get married yet, and they also knew that the way Carol's character had developed she only had eyes for Tom. She was too loyal and lovestruck to fall in love with someone else.

While I was off the show, the producers brought back the creator and original writer of the show, Irna Phillips. She had always liked "Carol" and decided that to boost the ratings she would start off with a big church wedding for Carol and Tom. I was back on the show, and Carol had her man and her happiness, but not for long.

More than anything else, Carol wanted to have children. But Tom, a struggling young law student, wasn't ready. He kept saying, "Wait until I get established." Repeatedly Carol's requests for a child always got the same answer. "This isn't the time." When Tom began a law practice, Carol finally got the answer she had waited for. "Sure, why not?" Tom said.

Carol's hopes for a family were destroyed when a doctor told her that she was sterile. From that time on she never felt completely fulfilled as a woman. She felt like the geranium plant she watered which would never bloom. Her life was filled with anguish. Even though Tom had no trouble accepting the situation, Carol felt she had let Tom down, and she would cry when she saw a child or baby-sat for a friend.

Meanwhile, Tom was becoming entangled with his very first client. Her name was Natalie, a beautiful, seductive girl who was trying to lure him into her web. But Tom didn't realize her scheming. In his enthusiasm to help her with her legal problems, he'd visit her at night, stay too long, and end up tip-toeing into his own bedroom when he got home.

Carol tried hard not to let this woman bother her. She even invited her over for dinner the night before her case came to trial. That same night, however, Tom drove Natalie home and didn't come back until morning, with the excuse that he "had to calm down her nerves." When Carol tried to reach out to Tom, to get him to understand what she was going through and to understand him, he responded by withdrawing. The more quiet he became, the more Carol suspected that Tom and Natalie were having an affair.

Her nerves shattered, she asked Tom for a divorce. In the weeks that followed, Tom won his case and Carol began to realize that she couldn't live without him. But it was too late. Just as she was seeking a reconciliation, Tom was growing more attached to Natalie. He told Carol, "We belong on our own." Soon after, he married Natalie and Carol was devastated.

The only things that kept her going were her job in the bookstore and Jay Stallings. Jay had come to town one day and had met her in the bookstore. Periodically he dropped by to see her, and he was always sympathetic to her problems and defended her position. He said that Tom had always treated her like a "doormat." One day Carol decided to get bold and break out of her "square" mold by taking the initiative with Jay. She invited him for dinner. They had a wonderful time, dancing to disco music, sharing a meal Carol had cooked. During the evening, though, she kept him at arm's length. Whenever he made a romantic advance, she brushed him off.

After he left that night, Carol was overcome by the emptiness of the room and the loneliness of her life. But Jay had calculated her mood. He had left his keys in the couch and had to come back for them. When he did, Carol was ready for his love.

But the fans weren't ready. They couldn't imagine that Carol could have an affair. She wasn't the type. Letters poured into the show: "Carol would never do something like that—she's too good." As a result, the writers had Carol go to New York, where she and Jay eloped. Through the marriage, the writers hoped to redeem Jay's character too—to make his intentions honorable and to show that he wasn't just a man who had been out for a fling with a naïve, vulnerable woman.

When they married, Jay Stallings was head of his own construction company. He was a stubborn, unaffectionate kind of guy and not many people liked him. He also had a wandering eye. First he got involved with Susan. He took her home one night when she was drunk. Then Natalie came on the scene again. She set her sights on Jay and ended up having an affair with him. When Tom found out, his marriage to Natalie broke up.

When Carol found out, at first she was devastated. Not only had Jay been unfaithful, but he had also gotten involved with the same girl who had taken away her first husband. But Jay kept asking for another chance and kept repeating how much he loved Carol. He didn't love Natalie, he insisted; it was just something that happened. Finally, Carol decided to forgive him. Whereas Tom had betrayed her by declaring his love for Natalie, Jay truly loved Carol despite his weak nature. And she forgave Jay, but despite Carol's love, Jay couldn't help himself. Natalie seduced him one more time. A few weeks later, Natalie discovered she was pregnant.

Carol was distraught. She could never have a child, and now, Natalie, the woman who had torn her life apart, was having Jay's child. Because Carol doesn't believe in abortion, she urged Natalie to have the child and offered to adopt the baby. Jay poured his money into helping Natalie for the sake of Carol and the unborn child. Right after the baby was born, Natalie left town with the baby.

For Carol and Jay, the loss of the baby precipitated more torment, more arguments. They fought over her desire for the baby and his cold, uncaring attitude. She decided to leave him for good. But again, Jay was redeemed when he saved "Annie" from being hurt by falling scaffolding and ended up in the hospital. Carol's heart went out to him when she saw him in pain, and they were united again.

Their newfound appreciation for each other was short-lived. A man was murdered, and Jay was the only suspect because he was visiting the man the day he was killed. He had left the man's house upset over an argument. From there, he went to his secretary's apartment to pick up some papers. Next door lived Melinda, a woman who had been making overtures to him. Because he was upset, he went to see her. He talked to her for a while, and in spite of her attempts to lure him, he went home to Carol.

Carol believed in Jay. She knew he couldn't have committed the murder. But Jay's only alibi was that he was with Melinda at the time of the murder. And he knew that if he confessed that to Carol it would end their marriage. So he lied to his lawyer, Tom Hughes, and to the District Attorney. Things looked bad for Jay until Tom found a pair of gloves at Melinda's and realized they belonged to Jay. He confronted Jay, who told Carol that he had been with Melinda. And the long-suffering Carol accepted Jay's explanation that he had just visited Melinda—nothing more. She believed him, until Melinda took the witness stand.

In court, Melinda, wishing to uphold her reputation, said that Jay forced himself into her apartment and attacked her. Her description freed Jay from jail as a murderer, but convicted him in the eyes of Carol. After Melinda's testimony, Jay looked around the courtroom and discovered that the only empty seat was Carol's.

Carol was suffering through the torment of another divorce proceeding when one day she opened the door and found a baby at her doorstep. Natalie had decided to give up the baby, and the only way Carol could adopt "Amy" was to take Jay back.

The Stallings family had finally found happiness. Carol had her baby, Jay had his wife. The only dark cloud over their life was Jay's job. He had lost his construction company because of Natalie's financial demands for the baby. Now he was working for his old employee, Hank, who wanted to hurt Jay and who realized that the only way he could do it was through Carol. One day, when Jay was out of town on business, Hank attempted to rape her at the construction shed. When his first attempt failed, he attacked her again in the bookstore.

When Jay found out, he beat up Hank and was charged with assault. Through a surprising turn of events Hank went to jail as a result of an assault he had been involved in in Texas, but Jay was sentenced to a work farm for sixty days. Now came more tears for Carol with their separation and lack of money. Baby Amy became Carol's only source of comfort.

Sometimes I'm asked if I become Carol during these ordeals. My personality has had to merge with Carol's, and when I'm on the set, my mind has to let Carol's take over. One example was the time Carol tried to effect a reconciliation with her first husband, Tom, after asking him for a divorce.

"I've been doing a lot of thinking, and I realize how many things I've done wrong," Carol told Tom. "Maybe we can work it out."

But by then Tom had already been smitten by Natalie. "It's nobody's fault," he answered, "but I still think we belong on our own."

As he spoke those words, it felt like a knife had gone through me. I could feel the pain that Carol was going through. In my mind there was the inner dialogue that every actress has to have. I was thinking Carol's thoughts. "Why isn't he responding to me? Why doesn't he want to stay together?"

One of the funniest dilemmas I faced as Carol was playing opposite a new actor, C. David Colson, who stepped into the role of Tom just after Carol had asked for a divorce. I was in the kitchen on the set, making spaghetti, and in those familiar surroundings where I had "lived" for so many years, all the memories of my years with Tom came back to me. Suddenly, I found myself staring at a strange man who had walked into the room.

I wondered, "What is this guy doing in my house?" It was the new Tom, and it took me a while to adjust to arguing with him, just as it took the audience a while to get used to seeing him in the role. I enjoyed working with C. David, who nick-named me "doormat." One summer he, Judith Chapman, who played Natalie, and I sang and read poetry in a production of "The World of Carl Sandburg." Len Valenta, our director from "As the World Turns," also directed us in the produc-tion.

Fans will often ask me if the crying scenes are real or if I use onions. Believe me, the tears are real and we don't use gim-micks. When Hank attacked me in the shed, it wasn't a phony fight. Hank threw me across the room, and I hit him on the head with a break-away bottle, designed to come apart on im-pact. But I still got bruises on my arms, and Hank got a cut on his ear because the bottle, which is made of a sugar solu-tion, had some ragged edges.

But the times when Carol's life overlaps most with mine are during bedroom scenes. I always like Norman to watch the show so that he can give me advice on how I did the scene. I take care to warn him when a bedroom scene is coming up. It's not that he's jealous. He knows I love only him. It's just that it's hard to see someone you love being close to anyone else.

"We have to kiss in this one," I warned him once a few minutes before the show came on. I went into the bedroom to set my hair while Norman watched the show. He had his checkbook on his lap and was calculating his balance while he watched.

About ten minutes into the show I heard a groan from the living room. "This is the fifth time I've tried to balance this account and I have to do it over." We both smiled to our-selves, knowing why.

No matter how closely my life and Carol's are intertwined, there are some obvious differences between us. A big difference is Norman. When I look at Carol's life, and see her burdened by a weak husband with few moral standards to guide him, I know how blessed I am to have a strong, faithful, and loving husband like Norman. He's my spiritual guide, my professional adviser, my lover, and my best friend. And I've come to trust his judgment implicitly. I've even got a saying around the house: "Norman knows." And I know that whenever I'm feeling low or facing a problem, he'll be there to back me up one hundred per cent.

Often when I'm at work I'll sigh and say, "Oh, I miss Norman."

Someone will say, "When did you see him last? Is he away?"

"No," I reply. "I saw him this morning, but that seems like a long time ago." I feel very much without him when we're apart.

When it comes to my career, Norman is my best critic. And even when he's watching those romantic scenes he has grown to where he can detach himself from his own emotions to give me an objective appraisal of my performance.

If he is my best critic, he's also one of my best directors. Because he's a minister, he's used to preaching and putting across points in a sermon. As a result, he can understand many of my acting problems, particularly when I'm trying to conceptualize a scene and figure out what kind of mood to project.

He was driving me to work one morning when I was working on my lines. Hank had attacked me in the bookstore several scenes before. Now the scene called for me to be waking up in my apartment as my friend Laurie was asking me if I wanted breakfast.

"I have a suggestion," said Norman. "Why don't you do this scene differently? You've been dazed all week as a result of the attack. Instead of being dazed in the morning too, why don't you play up being physically worn out and exhausted?"

As Norman drove through the traffic, he said, "Think about what you're like in the early morning. Sometimes the day after a hard show you're so tired you can barely think. Look at the scene this way: You've been at the point of exhaustion for days because of the attack. Now that you're finally getting some sleep, you go into a deep, deep sleep. You're not dazed in the morning. You're just too tired to think about anything. Your body aches and you can hardly respond to Laurie's suggestion. Take advantage of the way you feel every morning, when you sit on the edge of the bed really dead."

After a few minutes I had lulled myself into a stupor, and then drowsily I looked up at Norman.

"That's it," he said.

After he saw the scene on TV he was beaming. "You did it! You looked just like you do some mornings—no makeup, hair messed up, really out of it."

There's an almost tangible strength I get from Norman when I'm at work, and that's the confidence of knowing that he supports me and respects my ideas. When I was young, my father would always say, "I've got the fullest confidence in you." And that's exactly the kind of feeling I get from Norman.

Because we discuss my scripts together in advance, when I go to the studio and have a disagreement with the director over a scene I don't have to worry about his reaction. I've already gone over with Norman what I want to say, so my thoughts are clear and I can back them up. In the past I often stated my views, but because I was strongly opposed or didn't express myself clearly I would end up retreating. And I'd be frustrated at myself for not being able to explain my point of view.

Norman has made me see that there's a time to speak up at the risk of not being agreed with, especially when I have a point I think is important. He's made me feel that my opinions count, and he's made me feel very important. When it comes right down to it, that's the way God wants each of us to feel. And I believe He's given me Norman to help me learn that lesson.

Norman is always there, ready to pray with me and to calm me down when I call him from work, tense over an audition or upset by a difficult day. Even when he's not at home, sometimes just hearing his voice on the answering machine is comforting enough. When I leave a message, it's reassuring to know that he'll hear it, and that in some way we've made contact.

At times I've been close to tears when I've picked up the phone to call. As soon as I hear his gentle voice I feel better immediately. Sometimes Norman will tell me a Bible verse to lift my spirits, or he'll pray. "God, I can't be there with Rita on the set, but You can. We know she's had this disagreement. Please help her try to understand the other person's point of view, and help him to see hers."

Along with the strength I get from Norman there's an even bigger difference between Carol Stallings and me. I'm a Christian; Carol isn't. I can turn to the Bible for guidance and feel God's love and comfort.

But as a Christian, I admire Carol's capacity for forgiveness, such as the time she adopted Natalie's and Jay's baby. Although she sometimes seems like a "doormat" in her willingness to take Jay back time after time, to me it seems like the right thing to do. People may say she should get rid of Jay, but because of Carol's inner strength and fortitude I feel she ends up on top. After all, she now has a devoted husband who loves her, a baby she's always wanted, and a solid family life. I think that many a lonely woman would like to be in her place.

As for my reaction if Norman ever went with other women, let's just say that I get jealous when he talks to the operator! But he always builds me up and makes me feel I'm the only one in the world for him. So I can't put myself in Carol's place.

Every day, at home and on the job, the fact that I have Jesus to turn to gives me the ability to face problems no matter how difficult they may seem. My working day can be long and taxing. It takes an entire day to tape a show, from seven in the morning until about seven at night. I'm up at 5 A.M. on the two or three days a week that I go to the studio. The first thing I do is set my hair so that I have one less thing to worry about at work. I keep my hair up in curlers until about an hour before taping.

As Norman is driving me to work, we pray together, and I ask God, "Lord, help me see the needs of the people at work today. Help me not to think of myself, but to be open to others."

By seven I'm in the rehearsal hall with the other members of the cast to go over our "blocking," the movements—walking, fighting, opening doors—that correspond to our lines. The room is big and bare, with only a few tables and chairs to represent props. Two hours later we repeat the scenes so that the cameraman and director can plan the best camera angles for each line. That's followed by a run-through of the scene and notes from the director and producer on how to improve our performance. In between these run-throughs there's the wardrobe room to go to for costumes, the makeup room to run to, and mini-rehearsals with other actors as we're getting our hair done or putting on makeup. Tensions are always running high.

Often, the tensions are the greatest in the wardrobe room. That's probably because we all care about how we look. The studio has a lot of designer clothes, from designers like Dominic Rompollo, who makes the First Lady's clothes. But often the dresses the wardrobe women have chosen for me end up not fitting well or not being something I feel comfortable in. If I have a new outfit of my own that I like I might ask to wear my own clothes. What gets frustrating is trying on one of the studio's chic high-fashion dresses and finding out that it hangs down to my ankles or that it just isn't "me." Then there's the scramble to have it altered right away or find something else. They also keep a few dresses to use as standbys for me, and I'm always amazed at their patience in wanting us to look just right.

By twelve we're ready to tape the first half of the show. By two-thirty we begin again with the whole routine of blocking, camera blocking, rehearsals and taping for the second half. That lasts until about seven.

With all the rush, and with the frenzied pace of remembering lines, checking makeup, watching my blocking, and having my clothes right, I try to remember that God is in control. I pray quietly before the camera starts rolling, and God gives me the peace of knowing that whatever happens is in His hands.

But it's been in my relationships with other people at work when God has given me the most important cues in my acting career. One morning several years ago I was performing on another soap opera and was having difficulty working with another actor. He was very tense and kept snapping at me. We finally got into a situation that blew up. I knew we couldn't go on working like that. And I knew it was my place as a Christian to make the first move. God isn't interested in our sticking up for our own rights or defending ourselves. He knows who's done what, and the Bible says to leave everything up to Him. Psalm 37, for example, tells us "your innocence will be clear to everyone. He will vindicate you with the blazing light of justice" (*The Living Bible*). It's up to us to reach out.

So, I bought some dried fruit and nuts at a health food store, put them in a bag, and gave it to the actor. I put my hand on his shoulder and apologized for anything I had done to hurt him.

"We work too well together to let anything come between us. This is just a little something to say, 'Let's start again.'"

He was very responsive, and we were able to make the scenes work better than ever.

It's no secret at "As the World Turns" that I'm a Christian, and that I want others to share the happiness I've found in Jesus. And often people I haven't talked to about Christ have gotten the message.

A new actress came to the show as an extra, and as we struck up a conversation it turned out that she was a Christian too. We had so much to talk about it seemed as though we had known each other for years. Although she was new on the set, she was quick to make friends and very open about telling people about Jesus.

Later that day, the stage manager, a big burly guy with a cowboy hat, came up to the two of us and asked, "Are you two sisters?"

"No, but we're in love with the same person and neither of us minds," she said.

He looked at her, then he looked at me, and with a twinkle in his eye said, "Jesus, right?" I never thought he'd make that connection. I don't remember ever speaking to him directly about my faith, but he knew.

In my own way I try to let others know about God's love, but I'm never sure how effective I am. A few years ago a woman I work with came to me in my dressing room. Her heart was troubled by an argument she had had with someone.

"Would you please say a prayer for me?" she asked.

"Why don't we pray right now?" I said. We prayed, and I had just finished reading some Scripture verses when I got the feeling that she had drifted off and was thinking about something else. Abruptly, she said goodbye.

I thought, "Lord, why do You use me at all? I'm no good at this."

Later that day, the woman came up to me and said, "You know what really helped me was something you wrote on a piece of paper several weeks ago. You wrote, 'Your love of God is measured by the love you have for your greatest enemies.' Oh, did that help me! I went over to the person I was angry with and was as nice to her as I could be."

God had used something I had forgotten about to help this woman out.

I've found that even small incidents on the set can turn into an opportunity to talk about God. One day I accidentally bumped into a camera and hurt my side. Under my breath I said, "Praise You, Lord."

The cameraman overheard me, and he thought I was being sarcastic. "Do you think that's the kind of thing you should say?" he asked.

This gave me a chance to explain Romans 8:28: "And we know that all things work together for good to them that love God, to them who are the called according to His purpose" (King James).

"As a Christian," I explained, "because I've asked the Lord

to take my whole life into His hands, no matter what happens God's in control. He has allowed it to happen.

"It's during those times of trouble that I really have to trust the Lord. My whole life is in God's hands, and no matter what comes into it, I should give thanks.

"When I get depressed, I believe Satan has a victory. So if I say, 'Praise the Lord' when something bad happens, in my mind I picture Satan defeated. It's like giving him a punch in the stomach."

The cameraman listened attentively to what I had to say. A little later, I realized how well he had listened. I forgot a line, and said, "Ooops."

He stuck his head out from behind the camera and said, "Praise the Lord!"

"You're right," I said. "Praise the Lord!"

But even more important than talking about God is trying to show others that God has made a difference in my life. He has given me an example through Norman of how wonderful it is to be able to count on someone. That's the kind of feeling I want to give other people—that they can count on me. I want to surround them with positive feedback and help create a work environment that doesn't have any hassles. When someone is nervous about remembering lines, I want to encourage that person. "You'll get it, you always do." That's the strength I get from God through Norman.

One of the toughest days I've had on the set was during the rape sequences, when Hank, who was played by Kipp Whitman, attacked Carol in the bookstore. They were physically grueling scenes and technically difficult to shoot. After we taped the scene, Kipp and I would keep holding the mood while we waited to see if the director and producer "bought" it. But a few times we heard, "I'm sorry folks, but we need to do it again." It wasn't my place to complain. Instead, I tried to be as positive as possible. Retakes are part of my job as an actress, and from the Bible I knew that I was working for God and I wanted to do my best.

We had to do the scene over and over again. And I tried to keep my spirits up.

The next day, the director said, "You did a fantastic job." I thanked him, then he added, "I don't just mean your acting; I'm talking about your attitude."

I thought to myself, "That's what it's all about," and I thanked God that He had given me a good attitude.

It's funny how God can use even a bedroom scene to affirm the most important part of my life—my marriage. Acting in a bedroom scene is far from the romantic interlude that appears on the screen. To begin with, the mood in the studio is technical and fast-paced. We're concerned about getting our lines right and getting the right mood.

The set itself is wide open, with only one wall behind the bed to simulate a room. There's no intimacy at all because the studio is filled with people. There are three cameramen, two teleprompter holders, two boom men holding the mikes, two stage managers, several propmen, plus carpenters and electricians.

Typical is the scene that Dennis Cooney, who plays Jay, and I did right after Carol and Jay were reconciled. We got into bed, and, to break the awkwardness, Dennis said, "Boy it's been a long time since we had a scene like this."

What was even more awkward was trying to get comfortable. In order for the camera to see our faces, we were both propped up with lots of pillows. I looked like I had a double chin. From the angle I was in, I had to strain to look into Dennis' face.

The cast of "As the World Turns" is like a big family. We all know each other well after all these years. As a result, everyone knows Norman and they know how much I love him. Even when he's not there he's a part of our studio family. So when Carol and Jay have a scene in bed, Norman is on everyone's mind.

"Tell Norman I was fully dressed under the sheet," quipped Dennis.

And one of the cameramen exclaimed, "Boy, Norman is a lucky guy."

After the scene, the tears had come, the director had gotten the shots he wanted, and over the loud studio intercom a voice boomed loud and clear: "Okay, Rita, you can go home to Norman now."

10

"Don't Call Me Mr. Rita"

Every television in the department store displayed a closeup of Rita performing a dramatic scene on the show. Not every husband can spend a moment with his wife simply by making his way to the television section of a store. Often as I pass a newsstand on the street or in the subway I see Rita smiling at me from the cover of a TV magazine.

But on this particular day, as I watched Rita on the store's TV, a nicely dressed older lady came up and stood beside me. For several minutes, we stood quietly together, enjoying the show. When a commercial came on, she turned to me and said, "Do you watch soap operas too?"

"Well," I said, "the girl who plays Carol Stallings is my wife."

Her face fell deadly serious. "You don't mean it."

"Yes, I do," I said.

"You don't mean it." Her face was still deadly serious but the feather in her hat seemed to twitch.

"Yes, I do," I repeated.

"Oh my . . . oh my . . . wait till I tell all my friends that I met you. They'll never believe it."

This was my first experience as a husband with one of the millions of fans of Rita and "As the World Turns." Believe me, it restores my faith in television and the people who watch it to meet and correspond with some of these folks.

Of course, there are times when being the husband of a celebrity can be trying. One night we were sitting in a restaurant and a lady passed by shouting, "Her Carol, does your husband Jay know you're out with another man?"

With that she just kept on walking, leaving us surrounded by staring customers.

Once in a crowded airport a lady came up to us and quietly asked Rita, "Are you really who you look like?" Rita politely nodded yes.

"It's her, George!" she shouted across the big room. "It's Carol on 'As the World Turns.'"

I still shake my head when I think of a worship and praise service that Rita and I attended. While everyone was looking to heaven and praising God, a lady came up to Rita, embraced her, and asked what was going to happen next on the show. She was so caught up in the show she just didn't realize that this was our moment to share with the Lord.

I can laugh at stories like these now because unpleasant experiences are rare and no harm is intended. But I still wonder about something that happened one night in the Americana Hotel.

Rita and I were invited to a dinner in the huge ballroom. When we came in, we tried to get acquainted with a lady at our table. She seemed cool and unfriendly and all but ignored us. Then she found out Rita was on television. At that point, she began to overflow with conversation. She questioned Rita on every facet of show business and requested her autograph. Several times during the evening she brought friends from other tables to introduce them to Rita.

I knew this lady was monopolizing my wife, but I also

knew the excitement of meeting someone famous. Finally, she directed a single question to me.

"Do people call you Mr. Rita?"

I tried to think of something smart to say, but nothing came out. I felt embarrassed, I felt rage, and I felt hurt, but I just sat there looking at her.

"No," Rita said smiling confidently. "They call me the pastor's wife." With her eyes she was saying, "Nobody puts down my man."

Sometimes a fan will walk up to Rita absolutely starstruck, unable to notice anyone else, even when Rita introduces me as her husband. When this happens often, I can begin to feel left out, especially when I've been used to being introduced as the "pastor." I've tried to learn not only to understand this reaction of fans but to identify with it as well.

I'll never forget the night Rita introduced me to Jack Dempsey. The former world champion boxer smiled at me gently and extended the huge right hand that knocked out many a young fighter. I guess I was pretty starstruck myself and unable to notice much else. I did make sure to respectfully greet and talk with his wife, though!

Since then, Rita has introduced me to a host of celebrities. And let me tell you, meeting some of America's best friends never becomes commonplace. One day as we walked along Broadway, I recognized the young man walking toward us as "John-Boy" of "The Waltons."

"Richard Thomas," Rita called out, happily surprised.

"Rita, how are you?" he said. I didn't even know they had met, but there they were obviously good friends.

"I want you to meet my husband, Norman."

He greeted me enthusiastically and said, "Listen, my wife and I are in New York for a while, maybe we can get together."

Whenever a fan walks up to Rita with a blank look—except for eyes the size of silver dollars—I remember that day and I understand.

I guess the question I'm asked the most is, "What does it feel like when your wife does kissing scenes?"

Rita and I were in Asbury Park, New Jersey, when I first saw her in a kissing scene on TV. We had gone to the Jersey Shore for a quiet day together, just the two of us. It was off-season so the boardwalk was pretty empty. The beach was deserted and the rides and amusements were like an incredible ghost town. The sun was bright, the air was cool, and we seemed to have the ocean all to ourselves.

After a long walk, we stopped into the only luncheonette open on the boardwalk. We were the only customers. When we asked if they had a television, they produced a dusty old portable from the back and sat down to watch the show with us. They got so excited when Rita actually came on that I had to smile.

As we watched together, Rita moved into the arms of Dennis Cooney, Jay on the show. Then they kissed and no one in the tiny restaurant knew how to react.

We walked back to our car, and I was in a bad mood. I knew I was being silly, but it didn't lift my spirits. I was impatient with Rita and edgy. Finally I asked myself, "Is that silly scene bothering you?" Everything in me said, "You're darn right it is."

In those first few months without the ministry, Rita was the only thing between me and rock bottom. When I saw her kissing another man, I felt separated from her. Apart from Rita and the Lord, I was nothing.

But Rita saw my need and embraced me with the love that only a person in touch with Christ can give. And many times during the next few months, I needed that love, desperately.

I remember the first telethon Rita and I did together in Virginia for the March of Dimes. We had started making some outside appearances together at telethons and banquets, and from our point of view we operated as a team. For this telethon, we had set aside the weekend to fly down to Virginia and donate our services, and we were excited by the chance to work together.

Everyone welcomed us warmly. I opened the program with a prayer, then Rita gave her testimony. We sang together, and throughout the evening the emcee handed the mike back and forth between Rita and me. The program lasted throughout the night, and it was dawn when we finally dragged ourselves exhausted to our hotel room.

The morning paper was already there, and when I picked it up the first thing I saw was Rita's picture. I was thrilled to see that we had gotten some publicity, but as I read through the article, my enthusiasm waned. There wasn't one word about "us" in the entire article—not even a mention that I was at the telethon and shared in the program.

For the first time since I had left my church a few months before, I struggled to hold back the tears. It wasn't that I just wanted recognition. It was the fact that Rita was so proud of me and made me a part of everything, but I was obviously quite forgettable to everyone else.

My emotional letdown was too great, and I was simply too tired to sort out my feelings. I stopped fighting the tears.

Rita couldn't understand why I was so low. "You did a great job, sweetheart," she said. "Your preaching was power-ful—the people loved you."

To me it was the final blow. I was tired of pretending. I told myself, "I'm nobody."

But through these rocky times of doubt and indecision, God gave me something more precious than fame or popularity. He gave me Rita. She was the one who helped hold the pieces of my fragile ego together, who nourished my faith and brought me back to life. She was my minister, my friend, my biggest fan.

It could have been difficult—sometimes hell on earth—to be married to a soap opera star. But she made it heaven on earth. She never made me feel like "Mr. Rita." She made me feel like a man, and she made me feel secure in our love and in our life together.

One day I was sitting at the dining room table paying the bills when Rita returned from work. I had paid the check for her theatrical union dues and the bills for her clothes. But when I came across a bill for a suit I had bought for myself, I cringed. "This is coming from Rita's money," I thought.

When she came home, I said casually, "I know you don't feel this way, but sometimes I feel that I should be carrying my load."

With that, her eyes flashed. I had never seen her so angry.

"I know what you're going to say," I said. "We both make the money."

"That's right," she said. "That's *our* money. You are the head of this house and what you contribute to people's lives as a minister is priceless. If this is the way you're going to feel, how can you expect me to feel right about my working?"

At that moment I realized that the only way I could get Rita to calm down was to say—and mean it—"It's our money."

She didn't just build me up when we were alone. Repeatedly she boosted me when we were with other people. The fans were crowding around us one day and as usual a woman was giving her full attention to Rita and ignoring me.

"Did you see Annie and Beau's wedding on the show?" Rita asked.

"Why yes, it was beautiful," she answered.

"Did you know that Norman played the part of the minister?"

The woman turned to me excitedly and started asking questions about the show.

No matter where we were or how tired she was, Rita was always ready to support me. She would come home at night, weary from a day on the set, and still have the energy to lift my spirits. When she walked through the door, it was as if she had been given a shot of the most powerful drug in the world. The tiredness would leave her face, the weariness of the day would drift away, and she would give me one hundred per cent of her enthusiasm to pull me out of the pit.

I was feeling down one afternoon as I pondered my future. My career still wasn't going anywhere, and I was still caught between thoughts of the ministry and an acting career. Rita understood what I was going through even better than I could. But instead of chastising me, she gently and lovingly directed me to the Lord.

"Norm, the Lord is in control," she said. "If we really believe that the Lord gave us everything we have—our careers, our marriage—then if He takes something away, He can restore it. He can destroy the temple and in three days build it again."

When she said that in her positive way, I couldn't help seeing that my problem was a good old-fashioned lack of faith. And I began to realize that if God had taken my ministry away He would replace it with something better. He had brought us through the trials with my church, and as a result He had brought me closer to Rita. And step by step, God began to fill my life with new opportunities to serve Him.

First there was the chance to volunteer as an assistant pastor at a church in Manhattan. It wasn't a comfortable church in the suburbs with two assistants working under me like before. I was low man on a totem pole of four other ministers. But for me it was a dream come true. I traveled by bus and subway to the hospitals and nursing homes of the parish. God had put me back in my element and I felt like a real part of the city that I loved so much. More importantly, I was serving the Lord. I was a minister again.

One morning a few months later, I received a call from my first church in Jersey City. I knew the church was growing and doing well under a new pastor—my father. They were aware that I was committed to the church in New York, but they asked if I would consider coming back as an associate to help out for just a while. It was as though someone had turned the clock back ten years to when I was first called to that wonderful little church. Again I needed them and they needed me. With the blessing of the New York church, we said yes.

The first Sunday Rita and I returned to Jersey City was one of joy and tears. Everything was just as we had left it—the sanctuary, the stained-glass windows, and the love and respect of God's people. This was the place where I had baptized Rita one sunny August afternoon. That day seemed so long ago. So much had happened in between. God had brought us through the wilderness safely and now we were home.

In the weeks that followed, that great "Sunday morning feeling" came back to me. The confidence that I once had steadily returned. But it was clear that I would never be, nor did I want to be, the same as I was before God had given me a little more experience and a little more wisdom. He was shaping me, and I was better for it.

A little more than a year after our troubles began, the Lord revealed another piece to the puzzle. One night our friends Steve and Terrie gave us a surprise anniversary party. Among the guests were Ron Balsamo and his family. Ron was the young board member who had stood with us during the board meeting that resulted in our resignation. There were gifts and lots of food, and everyone was having a great time. Then Steve announced, "We have one more surprise, but we all have to get in our cars to do it."

Fifteen minutes later, we stopped outside of a little church. As I stepped inside, I realized what was happening. A few months before, a group of us had gone to see Steve in a play in Limestone Valley in Maryland. We met afterward in a beautiful country church and had talked about starting a fellowship together. We were all part of other ministries at the time, but our dream was to form a fellowship where we could meet together and do even more together for the Lord.

This was the place. This little church that Steve and Terrie had brought us to with our friends on our anniversary was the place we had built in our dreams. They had made arrangements for us to hold weekly services there. That evening was the beginning of Limestone Gospel Fellowship, a small group of people who were committed to God. God had not only restored my ministry, he had made me a pastor again, shepherding a flock. Limestone was the place where I could preach, and it was also to be the focal point for an expanded radio ministry.

As God was giving me new opportunities to work for Him in churches and groups like Limestone, He was also opening doors to a ministry through Rita's career. One night at a party I began to get a glimmer of what that ministry could mean.

Rita and I had gone to the home of an actress friend, and we met people from all areas of show business. There were actors, directors, stage designers—all gathered for an evening of fun. It was a lively, sophisticated crowd, and in the small apartment we sat in a close group having a kind of round-table discussion. Somehow the conversation drifted toward God.

"It doesn't really matter what you believe, we're all going to the same place," said someone in a lighthearted manner.

I was sitting quietly, listening to the conversation, when a woman leveled a serious question at me. "Do you believe that if you don't accept Christ you won't go to heaven?" she asked.

The room fell quiet. For some reason, all the other talking ceased, and everyone was looking directly at me, waiting for an answer.

In my mind I asked God for help: "Oh Lord, how can I pass up this opportunity? I can't just shrug off the question with an answer like 'There are many roads to God' when I believe there's only one way."

"I believe in the Bible," I told her. "And I believe that God is not willing that any should perish. God wants everybody to be with Him through eternity. But if you say you believe in the Bible, you have to believe in John 14:6, 'Jesus said to him, "I am the way, and the truth, and the life; no one comes to the Father but by Me."'"

I waited for the ceiling to cave in; for a torrent of angry, hostile comments to follow. But there was only silence. As I looked at the faces of the people in the room, I could see that they accepted me. They seemed to appreciate my sincerity. They didn't feel rejected by my words, but seemed open to what I was saying.

For the next half hour, I continued to speak, answering questions, probing their thoughts. It was as if I had a little pulpit in the midst of that living room, and was speaking to a very special congregation.

I had prayed to preach, and now I was preaching, not in a traditional church as I had imagined, but in a star's living room. And I soon found myself preaching before ever widening audiences inside and outside of churches, as invitations began to come for Rita and me. We were asked to appear on TV shows, at charity benefits, at soap opera festivals, and at religious retreats.

Our first major TV appearance together was on the religious talk show, "The 700 Club." Even though Rita is used to appearing before millions of people on TV, she usually has a script. This time, we had to speak off the cuff, and both of us were nervous. But a few months and several TV shows later, we appeared on "The PTL Club." By then we were relaxed and had a good thing going. We knew just how to bounce the answers off one another, how to play up each other's strengths, and how to jump into the discussion when the other was floundering.

The more we flew around the country to preach and give our testimonies, the more my eyes opened to an exciting new ministry God had set before us. He was adding another dimension to the ministry we had at Limestone and at Jersey City.

Since I had left my old church, I had gone down many roads in search of a career. But now, together with Rita, I had found the road to fulfillment as a preacher.

It all came together for me one Sunday in September 1978, in Harrisburg, Pennsylvania, where we had been invited to speak. We got there early, and the people were just beginning to enter the large auditorium. As we settled into our front-row seats, I wondered if many people would come out to hear us and if I would be too nervous to speak to them once they got there.

When it was time for the service to begin, the pastor opened with a hymn and then turned the service over to us. The congregation welcomed us with applause as we walked up the steps in front of the platform. When we reached the top, we turned around to face more than nine hundred people.

Right then I expected my teeth to begin chattering or my knees to cave in. But they didn't. And you know, it felt good. It felt real good. This day was a long time coming, and if the Lord had gotten us this far, He wasn't going to let us down now.

The first song we sang was one of our old standbys, "Heaven Came Down," which began, "Oh what a wonderful wonderful day, day I will never forget." It wasn't just easy to smile and look into the people's eyes as we sang—it was real. The most natural thing in the world at that moment was to overflow with God's love.

Too often when people see us standing up there smiling and praising the Lord, they think we've never had any real problems. "Sure, they're happy," they think to themselves. "I would be happy too if I were like them. They've got it made." So in each program, Rita and I take a moment to share our testimony and answer their questions. We tell them about the great love of God that makes us all celebrities in His eyes.

The large audience that we faced this particular morning, however, was somewhat different from what we were used to. This was a relatively new fellowship and most of the people were still enjoying a "first love" experience in Jesus. Their joy in the Lord was plentiful, but they harbored few illusions about Christian living. They knew that God's love, forgiveness, and salvation were a free gift by faith, but they also knew that real Christian living is never easy no matter who you are.

When the time came to preach the message, Rita quietly went back to her seat in the front row. A stillness came over the room as the Holy Spirit prepared minds and hearts for the Word of God. In those seconds before I spoke, I thanked God for His faithfulness. "Oh Lord, You've brought us so far. I'll always thank You for this moment."

My overwhelming joy was not just because I was standing before nine hundred people, but also because God had trusted me to feed all of these hearts which were so precious to Him. I stepped up to the pulpit and directed my voice toward the two microphones extending toward me.

"A lot of folks are tired of the same old thing on Sunday mornings. They want something different for a change." As my voice came over the room through the huge loudspeakers, I sounded more like a sports announcer than a preacher.

"The message that I have for you this morning has been around for two thousand years, but I want to tell you, in my life it's brand new." Some smiles and nods told me that they knew just what I was talking about.

"This morning, I want to speak to you about true joy, true discipleship, and truly knowing Jesus. My text is a familiar one, John 15:7–13."

God had taught me much that I could share with them about true joy. I had learned that the joy of knowing Jesus didn't depend on the circumstances of life. In fact, when the pathway of faith is the darkest, that's when His joy means the most. Hebrews 12:2 tells us that "for the joy that was set before him [Jesus] endured the cross." In the midst of failure, and rejection, and tears a Christian possesses a wellspring of abundant joy even as the tears continue to fall. When you walk with Christ, you're never a nobody.

Discipleship was the second point in my message that morning. And here again, I could speak from God-given experience. When mere men rejected me, I thought I'd never be a minister again. But as I sat sobbing and defeated, the Director of the whole universe came personally to assure me that I'd always have a job with Him.

God had used Rita to teach me two important things about discipleship. First, I saw in her that believing in God is one thing, but walking with Him every day in constant communion is really what being a disciple of Christ is all about. Ministers can fall into the trap of being "Sunday Christians" only. God also showed me through Rita's life that witnessing for the Lord is not just a good sales pitch—it's demonstration. I wouldn't buy a house or a car on just a sales pitch. I want a demonstration. What makes us think we can win hearts for the Lord without a real demonstration of His love and peace and joy in our lives?

The only way I can describe the varied expressions on the faces of the congregation is to say that they were with me all the way.

"The final portion of my message today is about truly knowing Jesus. This is an exciting subject, but first I want to turn to what I think is the saddest verse in the Bible. Matthew 7:22–23 talks about the end times when people said to Jesus, 'Lord, Lord did we not prophesy in Your name, and cast out demons in Your name, and do many mighty works in Your name?' And Jesus looked at them and said, 'I never knew you; depart from Me.'

"What a tragic thought it is that a person could stand before the Lord Jesus and say, 'Well, Lord, I witnessed every day, I gave them the old sales pitch for You,' and He would turn away.

"On that last day Jesus will say, 'You never walked with Me or wanted to spend time with Me. I loved you so much, but I never knew you; depart from Me.'

"Rita and I believe that we are living in the end times today. In the Old Testament God told Noah that a day of judgment was coming. The people laughed as Noah built his big boat in the middle of a land where it never rained. Then one day the rain began to fall.

"Today wars and rumors of wars continue, but now terrorist nations have atomic capability. The world is ripe for holocaust. Ten years ago, few people were familiar with the term 'born-again.' Now it is a common expression because of the worldwide spiritual renewal prophesied for the last days. The world is ripe for rapture.

"Lately, everyone is talking about flying saucers and UFOs. Sightings have been reported all over the world, but the Bible says we haven't seen anything yet! Luke, in Chapter 21, tells us that men will see things in the sky that will make their hearts fail them for fear.

"To Christians, God says 'and when these things begin to come to pass, then look up, and lift up your heads; for your redemption draweth nigh' [King James].

"My invitation today is perhaps to that one heart who is listening to this message—that one person who says, 'I realize now I really don't know Jesus. I know the sales pitch. I've been part of the Christian Church, but if I stood before the Lord today I wonder if He would say "I never knew you—depart from Me." '

"My appeal this morning is to those who say, 'I want to know Him. I want to be that disciple. And I don't want that end day to come and have the Lord say, "You did a lot, but I never knew you." '

"If you are that person today, I want to know who you are. I want to look into your eyes. With your heads bowed, if you feel you want Jesus in your life, and you want Him as your savior, then raise your hand and look at me. I want to pray for you."

Nine hundred heads bowed in that congregation. Everything was still. And then I saw a miracle taking place. The Holy Spirit moved across the room like a soft breeze rustling one tree and then the next. In an ordered progression around the room, hands went up. It started in the back of the congregation on the right as one, two, three hands were raised. Then it moved a few pews in front of them as four, five, six hands were raised. And then toward the front of the room with seven, eight hands, and across the aisle on the left side of the room from front to back, continuing for several minutes.

As the Holy Spirit reached down to grasp hold of each life, the pattern was the same. A person would come to a decision, his or her head would slowly tilt up, his eyes would fix on mine, and then his hand would raise ever so slowly. In his face I could see the struggle that was going on in his heart. Who knows, he may have been going to church all his life, or been a member of the Sunday School. But now he was confessing inwardly, "I really don't know Jesus."

Watching the Holy Spirit sweep across the congregation

gave me a tremendous feeling of humility. If there was one thing I had learned in the past few months, it was that Norman Walter couldn't do anything. I had been rejected by the world, and had been cast aside by men, and yet God could still use me.

With my heart filled with joy, I prayed, "Lord, I know what I am unable to do. And now I see what You are able to do."

11

"Be Subject to One Another"

I had always wanted a husband who would be the head of the family, the spiritual guide and strength. I learned early in our romance that Norman was the man I had been looking for all my life.

The first inkling I had of his inner strength and direction was at one of our first parties at the home of one of Norman's friends. When I had dated before, it seemed that the right thing to do at a party was to gradually separate from my date and get to meet the rest of his friends. That way he could be free to walk around and talk to everyone. I wanted to give a hundred per cent to my relationship with Norman, and part of giving my all, I thought, was getting to meet his friends.

At the party, I left Norman and moved around the room meeting people. By the end of the evening, we had finally gotten back together and were sitting with a group of people when one of the men asked, "Who did you come with?"

"I'm with Norman," I said.

I didn't think anything about it until Norman and I got in the car to go home.

"There's something I want to share with you," said Norman. "It's not really important . . ." And I knew that meant I'd better listen closely.

"Honey, I think it would be good if we're not too far apart when we go places together," he said gently. "We don't have to spend every minute with each other. But if we drift, let's always have a communication that says we're together. We can look across the room at one another, and sometimes come together, but let's always keep that eye contact and bond of love even if we're across the room."

As I listened to him, everything I had thought before about the proper thing to do just crumbled away.

"It sounds great to me," I told him. I realized that this was the kind of man I had always wanted. Here was this wonderful guy telling me that I was so important that he wanted to be in communication with me always.

During our marriage I've found that it's these bonds of communication, both physical and spiritual, that have drawn us even closer together. The more we're willing to share with one another, the more we grow together. Paul says in Ephesians, "Be subject to one another out of reverence for Christ." What he is saying to me is that we need to submit our own wills to our spouses'—to be willing to learn from them, to listen to them, and to love them enough to put them first in everything.

The first principle of communication that Norman and I have tried to follow is being willing to learn from one another. The more I've learned to listen to him, the more I've developed as a wife and as a person. For one thing, he has taught me how to relax. In the past, it somehow seemed wrong to me to have a day off with nothing to do but have fun.

Because of my work during the week, I get behind in so many things I have to do at home, such as cleaning, organizing, or corresponding. So when the weekends finally roll around, I feel guilty unless I make a list and start to go through it. The problem is, I get exhausted, time passes, and I end up getting nothing accomplished.

But Norman helped me to understand the value of relaxation. In the middle of some project that was going nowhere, Norman would stop me and say, "We're going for a ride in the country. Come on, you need it. You'll get this stuff done later." After a beautiful drive in the country, I felt the burdens lifting and I felt deeply refreshed. When we got home, I was able to tackle any job with new enthusiasm, and I got the job done twice as effectively.

I've also learned a lot from listening to Norman's sermons. One of the messages that come back to me time and time again is his teaching on giving burdens to God. When we have troubles, says Norman, we think we are supposed to lift them off our shoulders and give them to God. The problem is that a lot of the time we just don't have enough strength on our own to do it. Instead, what we need to do is ask God to lift us up above our problems into His presence. When we're in the presence of the Father, Son, and Holy Spirit, the problems at hand seem very small and we're able to trust Him for the answers.

That's why people who know the power of prayer never seem to be defeated by their problems.

I put Norman's words into practice one morning when I woke up in a terrible mood. I wasn't irritated about anything in particular, I just felt grumpy and grouchy and mad at the world. But then I thought of Norman's words, and I knew I needed to spend time with God. When you're in a bad mood, it's not easy to pray. But I wanted to pull out of it. So I made myself pray out loud. I started praising God, over and over again. "Praise You, Lord," and "Thank You, Lord," and "I love You, Jesus."

Gradually I felt a loosening of the bonds that were holding me down. I could feel God's love again. I felt open and loving and ready to start the day with a joy that "passeth understanding."

I've also learned from Norman an important lesson about

loving my own family. Even after we were married, my family had a hard time accepting us. I'd be having a normal conversation with my mother on the phone, and feel our relationship was beginning to heal, when all of a sudden there would be an argument.

After each call, I was so upset I felt as though my insides were turned upside down. At the same time, I realized what a burden my problems were on Norman. He was without a church, and without a certain future, and yet there he was ministering to me.

Christmas came just a few weeks after we got married, and Norman and I went off to Brooklyn with a car full of presents for my family. But when we got there, no one was home. My mother and younger brother had gone away for the weekend.

I knew she was going through an agonizing period of adjustment. She had lost my father just a year before, and now she thought she had lost me, after years of being so close. But being in that empty house at Christmas only echoed the hurt.

Phone call after phone call showed that we just weren't getting anywhere. I was finally ready to resign myself to the fact that it would never change and that she would never accept us.

"This is it—I can't take it anymore," I said to Norman. "I can't keep reaching out. It's no use." I felt I was being torn apart by my family, and had few resources left to devote to building my marriage.

But just as I was ready to sever all ties with my family, Norman calmed the storm.

"Don't do something you're going to regret," he said. "You're upset now and you're reacting because of everything you've been through. But you've got to keep those lines of communication open. You can't just break off with someone you love so deeply.

"For your own emotional well-being, it's all right not to call your family for a while," he assured me. "But don't close the door. God is going to take care of the situation. Put it in His hands. Now's the time for a period of waiting and healing. It's just going to take time."

A year passed without any real communication, and by the second Christmas I wondered if my mother was ready to share it with us. Nobody called. Nothing happened. David, home for Christmas vacation, visited us, and it was great to see him. It was sad not to be all together as a family, but I knew I was doing the right thing.

During that year our marriage had had time to grow and our ministry began to emerge. But my mother was often on my mind. In the past, when she had been my manager, I had called her two and three times a day. We always knew what the other one was doing. Now, for the first time, I didn't know what was happening to her. I didn't know what she was doing or how she was feeling.

"God, I don't know how she is, but You know," I prayed.

And Norman would tell me, "God is taking care of your mother. He loves her and is taking care of her just as He cares about us. Remember, your mother is an intelligent, attractive woman and I know she's got a full life ahead of her."

The seeds of love were planted with prayer, but it was several months before we began to come back together. In response to a letter I wrote, my mother sent me a letter saying, "The Holy Spirit will heal us."

And that's exactly what happened. We met once in a while for dinner and just talked about the present, not the past. As we talked together and learned more about each other, I discovered that my mother and I had both grown without each other during the months of separation. And I knew that those times apart were important. Although it hurt me to think that she was all alone, God used that time to help speed her adjustment to my father's death. Because I wasn't there, she had to reach out to other people. She became a lector at church, and people looked forward to hearing her read the Scriptures. Now she wasn't just someone's mother, but a woman with her own personality and talents. Her week became filled with activities—prayer groups, retreats, teaching Sunday School, and visiting friends. She became vibrant and alive—and younger than I had ever seen her.

As we both started reaching out to one another, God did heal us. And the third Christmas after our marriage was a gift straight from God. My mother invited us to Brooklyn for Christmas dinner, along with my brothers and Norman's parents. There was no tension at all that day—just a group of people enjoying each other's company. Within each of us was a craving to be a real family, and a desire to love each other.

The healing had taken place. And we were a family again, stronger and more devoted than before.

Throughout our marriage Norman and I have found that it's important not only to listen to what the other is saying, but also to listen with a "third ear" that hears *behind* the words, to pick up what is really being said and what the true needs are.

Once Norman and I were in the middle of a discussion over where to put our white file cabinets. To me, it was just an objective conversation. He suggested that we put the cabinets one way; I said, "I don't know, I think it would be better the other way."

The conversation went back and forth with me explaining my position and Norman explaining his. Finally, he blurted out in frustration, "It's obvious. If I say it should go this way, you say it should go the other way."

His statement surprised me. I hadn't realized how strongly I had been coming across. At that moment I realized that my husband needed much more than a debate. What he was really saying was, "I need you to say you're with me—that you care about me and value my opinion."

He may have been overreacting, but I could understand why. After all, Norman had had a position of respect and leadership as a pastor and, now that all of that was gone, it seemed that even his wife wasn't with him.

I began to realize the tremendous responsibility I have as a wife. When we discuss anything, whether it be crucially important or ridiculously simple, it's always important *not* to put each other down but to lovingly share and really listen to what the other is saying.

Now, when we find ourselves in the middle of a tense discussion, we've come up with a method to dissipate the tension, reconfirm our love, and see things in the right perspective. In the heat of the moment, one of us will call out "time." That's the signal for the other person to give five reasons why he or she loves you.

If Norman called "time," I'd stop what I was doing and start reeling off a list of reasons why I love him. "I love you because you are the most wonderful person I've ever known. I'm crazy about your dimples. You've got the greatest kisses . . ." Before we'd get to number 5, we'd both end up laughing and hugging.

A third principle of communication which has worked in our marriage is stepping into the other person's shoes.

Sometimes a failure to see the other person's point of view is what causes so many problems in a marriage. One thing about soap operas is that the viewers get to see both sides of a story. They can therefore understand both Carol's problems and Jay's problems and be sympathetic to both, whereas Carol and Jay have a hard time communicating. If each were able to know what the other person was going through, they might have a fighting chance. In fact, when Carol finally decides to really listen to Jay, she is able to understand him, forgive him, and save their marriage.

I think in our own marriage, if we could know our spouse's feelings, and try to understand what he or she is going through, then we might realize that some of the problems could be solved if we're patient and sympathetic. One fan told me that her daughter's marriage was held together because of Carol's example on the show. When she saw that Carol forgave Jay, she realized that she could try to forgive her own husband for his mistakes. She had always admired Carol, and as she watched Carol's marriage grow back together, she was inspired to try to bring that same healing into her own life.

Norman and I make a conscious effort to step into each other's shoes in the middle of a problem we're facing. That happened right after we made a decision to try to start a family.

Norman had given his okay that it was time for us to have a child, and I was thrilled. In a sense, I felt like Carol did after finally hearing from Tom that the time was right to have a baby. Carol had wanted a child from the minute they were married, but Tom had repeatedly told her, "We don't have enough money, let's wait." With Norman and me, it wasn't the money. It was a matter of timing, because we had so many career obligations with my work and our ministry together.

But one day we were coming home from a party at Dennis Cooney's, when Norman said, "I think it's time we had our own children."

I was overjoyed. I raced out to buy all the books I could find on pregnancy and raising children. I went on a diet and eliminated all artificial sweeteners, sugars, and caffeine from our food. I was going to be as ready as I could be.

Like Carol, my whole life was wrapped up in the "project." I had calculated the best time to conceive, and was preparing for the big moment. But as the day came closer, Norman didn't seem to be part of the project. He wasn't his normal energetic self.

Saturday was "the day," according to my calculations. It was a very busy day, filled with shopping and visiting friends and an evening out in the city. When we got home, we got ready for bed, and I was so happy that we would be starting a new phase of our life together.

"Honey, what are you thinking?" I asked.

"It's not important," Norman said. "I was just thinking—this is a big step, our having a baby."

As I heard him voice his reservations, I started to fall apart. So often, God had spoken through Norman, and now I thought that God was telling us to wait.

"What are you thinking about?" he asked. I couldn't begin to tell him. I was so disappointed, and the question itself seemed absurd. He knew how much I wanted a baby—why did he even need to ask?

"I understand what you're saying—that we should wait to have a baby," I said. "But I can't handle it." And I started to cry.

"You're overreacting," he said.

Then I really got upset. How could he think I was over-reacting? How else could I act under the circumstances? I wanted to disappear under the covers. But Norman pushed the discussion further, and asked me to say out loud what he was feeling.

"Why don't you tell me what I'm trying to say," he said.

Although it hurt me to say it, I tried to express what he was thinking. "You're saying that it was a good idea to have a baby, but maybe right now is not the best time because of my heavy schedule with the show and because of our outside commitments. So we should wait a few months."

But it turned out that I had misunderstood what Norman was thinking. He thought the time was right. But because he was human, he had doubts and a moment of weakness. He was concerned about things that I hadn't thought of and needed my reassurance.

What would happen if "As the World Turns" decided to write Carol out of the script? My contract would be up soon, and there were many cast changes taking place. Also, would the show want to work around a pregnant actress? He was also concerned about how he could support a family with our high New York rent and expenses.

When I was able to understand his feelings, I told him it was right to wait until we found out more about the contract. I could understand the need to be responsible, and I was sure Norman would be glad that I agreed with him.

But he was deep in thought.

When he looked up at me, his whole expression had changed.

"I've been trying to figure out everything on the basis of my strength alone," he said. "How would I ever be able to support you and a baby if you were unable to work? You'd think I'd know by now that if God brought a baby into our life, He would provide one way or another. I believe that now the time is right and we should start a family, trusting in God's perfect timing."

I was glad to hear what he said. We knew God was our source and that He would take care of us. That same week, the show asked to renew my contract. Not only would they be glad to work around a pregnancy, but they would even consider writing it into the script!

By trying to put ourselves in each other's shoes, we were not only better able to understand each other's point of view, but we were able to get an even better understanding of our own.

In our marriage, we really believe in the biblical principles of submission and love. The fifth chapter of Ephesians says that wives should submit to their husbands and respect and honor them. Husbands have the profound responsibility of giving leadership and love, according to verse 25: "Husbands, love your wives, as Christ loved the church and gave Himself up for her."

I've found that when I can openly complement my husband and support his decisions, he can more effectively take on the responsibilities of being head of the house. I wanted a man I could look up to and love. And God gave me Norman.

We want to love each other as Christ loves us—totally, and without conditions. When you're both concerned more with giving than receiving, you've planted the seeds for a happy and fulfilling marriage.

12

NORMAN'S STORY

"The Two Shall Become One"

In one incredible year, God had restored our whole world and made it better than we had ever dreamed possible.

He had shown everyone around us that our marriage was His and that He would protect and sustain it. Our traveling ministry continued to grow with God's blessing as well. We sang our songs and shared God's word with seven hundred people, then nine hundred, then three thousand! Each time, the Lord miraculously kept my knees from shaking out from under me, and, praise His name, many came to a saving knowledge of Jesus.

Another reason that we'll never forget that year is that God had taken me, a weeping, defeated shell of a man, and restored my spirit and ministry. Pastoring a flock for the Lord is so much a part of me that I would often thank God for keeping me sane through all our trials. I learned that human faith is nothing when put to the test. The only faith that will see us through is that which we receive in fellowship with Christ.

The Limestone Gospel Fellowship, within a month of its founding, had the resources to support the first program of a radio ministry. The fellowship itself was just a handful of hard-working Christians, but it was already bearing fruit in God's kingdom.

The Lord works in strange and wonderful ways. Seven years before, as a young man entering the ministry, I had asked God, "Lord, do You want me to stay with a small congregation that I know and love, or should I seek a position where I could one day minister to hundreds or even thousands?" The Lord had now given us both of these.

On the second date Rita and I discovered that we shared a favorite verse, Ephesians 3:20. Truly, God kept the promise of that Scripture by blessing us, "infinitely beyond our highest prayers, desires, thoughts or hopes" (*The Living Bible*).

Who could ask for more? The answer is anyone who believes that God really loves them and cares about their lives. I believe He wants us to pray big prayers and keep them coming. In Philippians 4:6, He tells us to "pray about *everything* . . . and don't forget to thank Him for the answers" (*The Living Bible*). The more we rely upon Him, the more He'll increase our opportunities to serve Him.

This was never more clear than in the story of our first record album. A wedding reception was given for us six months after we eloped. And in our search for Christian music that would really touch hearts at the reception, we met a young couple whose gospel album had been a real blessing in our home. That was the beginning of our friendship with Mickey and Becki Moore.

At the reception we received so many gifts that Mickey and Becki offered to follow us back to our apartment with the gifts in their van. That night they stayed until 3:30 A.M. talking and sharing with us the many blessings of God in their lives. A few weeks later on their anniversary, Rita baked a cake for them and later that evening the four of us had devotions together. Almost apologetically, we told them that although we weren't singers, we, too, would like to record an album of the songs we sang as we traveled. They encouraged us and offered any help they could give.

A few weeks before they were to go out on a singing tour, God began speaking to us very definitely about Mickey and Becki. He assured us they were His anointed servants and that we should help to support their ministry. We were also led to ask them if, in addition to their already impossible schedule, they would help us publicize and book our appearances. They answered without blinking an eye, "We were just thinking about this very thing and we believe we can help you." With their help, a steady stream of new bookings came in for our ministry.

Even though we were so busy with the new ministry we had at Limestone, when Mickey and Becki left for their tour we missed their fellowship.

One Sunday as Rita dressed for church, she put a gospel record on the stereo. From the next room, suddenly I could hear this beautiful music. It was sweet and clear, sort of a combination of country music and gospel. All I knew was that the voice and the music blended into something that blessed my heart.

"Hey, Rita, that's my kind of music," I said. "Who is it?"

"It's Liz Humbard, honey. Isn't she great?"

"Who's Liz Humbard?"

"She's the daughter of Rex Humbard—you know—the evangelist."

I knew who Rex Humbard was because Rita watched his program on television each week as I prepared my message. But I had never heard of his daughter.

"Play it again, will you, sweetheart?" I said.

We played it again and again. The next week at the fellowship we played three songs from the album during the service. I can never remember enjoying any one record so much even in my days of rock 'n' roll!

Several weeks passed and Mickey and Becki returned from their tour with good news about even more bookings for us.

"And that's not all," Mickey said. "While we were away, I spoke with a Christian producer who's very interested in doing your album. His name is Larry Adams, and he produces Liz Humbard's music. Have you ever heard of her?" He had even brought a couple of Liz's albums for us to listen to!

Before long we were on our way to recording our album, *Becoming One,* with the title song written by Mickey and Becki.

God chose a winter weekend in Florida to perform one of His greatest miracles in our lives. We had been invited to speak at a "Sweethearts" banquet sponsored by the Full Gospel Business Men's Fellowship in Jacksonville. For our accommodations, they had chosen a hotel right on the beach. The last time we had been there we had stayed in that same hotel and loved it, so we were very pleased.

The banquet was a tremendous event with many coming forward to accept Christ or recommit their lives to Him. After I left to pray with those who had responded to the invitation, Rita was given the microphone. She called on couples who wished to renew their wedding vows to come forward. Again, many responded.

When we returned to our room, I fell asleep so quickly that the next thing I knew the phone was ringing with our wake-up call. Rita was up already so she picked up the phone and thanked the clerk at the desk.

It was like waking up on a ship. The windows and doors were closed, but you knew the ocean was out there, always moving. Room service brought coffee and eggs and my watch showed that we had ample time to dress for the service. After breakfast, Rita began to set her hair, so I took my coffee out on the balcony to finish it. Although the sky was gray and cloudy, the fresh warm air was a welcome change from the New York winter.

I could see across the beach and out onto the ocean. The wind and mist swept across the sand and palm trees.

"Lord, thank You so much for everything," I prayed. "We couldn't be happier, Lord, and we just want to give You all of the glory."

The aroma of the coffee in the fresh sea air made me want to stay on that balcony all day, but I knew it was time to go back inside and finish getting ready. Reluctantly, I closed the door and sat down on the bed. Rita came out of the bathroom and smiled.

"By the way, honey," she said, "a lady gave me a note for you after the service last night. Here it is."

I unfolded the paper and began to read. I'm not very good at reading people's handwriting, so it came out slowly.

"You are . . . on your way . . . to becoming a daddy!" At the bottom of the note, Rita had drawn a smiling face.

"You're kidding!" I said, dropping the note.

"No, I'm not, sweetheart. The test was positive."

"When did you find out?"

"I took the test myself this morning."

We embraced and laughed and cheered. There was no fear or doubt because when it's God's timing, you know it's right.

The next day a clinic confirmed her findings. We were parents-to-be.

Today we know in our hearts that whatever problems may lie ahead God will be our anchor through the storm. He has taught us that He can take every river Jordan, every wall of Jericho, and use it to build a stronger relationship with Him.

That's what we say in our ministry. We know it's a beautiful thing to walk with God, because we've done it. We've done it not only through the sunshine, but also through the shadows. It's summed up best in a short passage from the Book of James (King James):

"Blessed is the man that endureth temptation: for when he is tried, he shall receive the crown of life, which the Lord hath promised to them that love Him. . . .

"Every good gift and every perfect gift is from above, and cometh down from the Father of lights, with whom is no variableness, neither shadow of turning."

We have that crown of life that James writes about. We have the perfect gift from above. We have the assurance that God will never leave us.

The world may turn its back on us. Shadows may darken our lives again. But God, like a perfect sun which shines into every corner and crevice of our lives, will never turn away. With God, there will be no shadow of turning.

His light will shine forever.

WHAT DOES THE BIBLE SAY ABOUT THE END TIMES?

Don't You Think You Should Find Out?

____ **THE TERMINAL GENERATION**, Hal Lindsey, $2.50
In a chaotic, confused world that yearns for authenticity and validity, only the Bible remains as a constant source of hope and direction.

____ **RACING TOWARD JUDGMENT**, David Wilkerson, $1.95
Be aware of the signs that foretell the Judgment Day.

____ **THE HAPPIEST PEOPLE ON EARTH**, Demos Shakarian, $2.25
Down-to-earth story tackling questions of prophecy, guidance, and faith in God.

Order From Your Bookstore